You're Not Supposed To Be Here

Some of the Travels
    Some of the Views
        Some of the Life and
            Some of the Many Complaints
                of Ian Finkel

The World's Greatest Xylophonist

Ian Finkel

You're Not Suppose to Be Here
© 2010 Ian Finkel. All Rights Reserved.

All illustrations are copyright of their respective owners, and are also reproduced here in the spirit of publicity. Whilst we have made every effort to acknowledge specific credits whenever possible, we apologize for any omissions, and will undertake every effort to make any appropriate changes in future editions of this book if necessary.

No part of this book may be reproduced in any form or by any means, electronic, mechanical, digital, photocopying or recording, except for the inclusion in a review, without permission in writing from the publisher.

Published in the USA by:
BearManor Media
P O Box 71426
Albany, Georgia 31708
www.bearmanormedia.com

ISBN 1-59393-513-7

Printed in the United States of America.

Book and cover design by Darlene Swanson of Van-garde Imagery, Inc.

Contents

Introduction vii

The Hub of SHOWBIZ 1

Me. 9

A Home Boy in Dakar, Senegal 13

The Bells of Saint Petersburg, Russia 19

All Roads Lead to Rome, Italy 27

I'm Sittin' on Topkapi, Istanbul, Turkey 29

Getting Paid and "Negotiations" 33

Here's How I "Negotiate" 35

Dance of the Sugar PLUM 37

Names & Brains 43

The Green Spray 47

People Are the Same All Over the World. 53

The End of the Line 57

Ship of Fools At Sea 61

All This for $500 A Night 69

The Flying Dutchman 75

It's Raining Volkswagens 79

A Brunei-Guy 83

Beat Me Daddy Eight to the Bar. 91

Nut Training. 99

Bands That Should Disband 105

My Mentor 113

Under the Double Standard. 117

Team Comedy. 123

It's You, You, You 127

R-e-s-p-e-c-t 133

Exit Music 137

Dedication. 139

"To travel is to discover that everyone is wrong about other countries." – Aldous Huxley

"Except for me!" – Ian Finkel

"The show must go on!" – Old Theatre Saying

"Not at these prices!" – Ian Finkel

This page has been left blank so that the reader may have time to get a sandwich and espresso

Introduction

I never wanted the audience to love me. I have enough love in me to love myself for another lifetime. Their respect would be nice. After all, I've practiced my craft for thirty-six years and became the best at it. I do respect myself and certainly respect some others, like the guys who work at my favorite cigar store, but most of the time I get the feeling that when I make my entrance onto the stage and the audience sees me and my xylophone, I should open with the line, "I know, you see this thing and you hate me already!" So I have to work like a Saint Bernard to win them over.

This apple fell far from its tree with me. My entire family is a "love me, love me, love me" group and they need that love to exist. And, of course, they love their audience back . . . "madly" . . . and their successes prove it. Especially my father, Fyvush Finkel, the great actor, comedian and entertainer; he gives off his love like the beams of the Ambrose Lighthouse in the night. People love him as soon as they see him - nay, hear his name. And I must admit he is a saintly figure, never a bad word about anyone. Why, he'd do fifty shows a week for free if you'd let him.

Sometimes he tells me, "Last week I did great business."

"What do you mean?" I ask.

"I signed twenty-three autographs."

God, he counts them!

"And I lost seven handkerchiefs."

"What do you mean, seven handkerchiefs?"

"Well, when I take the bus to see my agent, God watch over him, people come to talk to me and sometimes they take a souvenir."

"You take the bus?!!!"

"Naturally, that way I get to meet in person all the wonderful folks that watch my show on TV."

"But some fans are nuts and could hurt you!"

"Nah, why would they do that?"

"Why? Because . . . some people are crazy! You should have a bodyguard."

"On the bus with me? We'd both need a seat."

"No, in a cab and . . . oh, forget it!!"

My father did instill a love of all forms of showbiz in me and when I finally figured out what I wanted to do, I went into it like a crazed tiger that has been released into the wild after being caged without food and water for a week. But by the time I "got good" at playing the xylophone, the whole shape of the music scene changed.

You see, Vaudeville died. But, like a Phoenix, with a whip cream pie on its face, it rose up from the ashes of legit and perched its claws on cruise ships. Before *The Love Boat* television show gave the cruise ship industry a new life, working as an entertainer on ships equaled a gig next to the two-headed goat in an old-time Coney Island sideshow. Performing on ships in the days prior to the 1970s meant you could not get a gig in a bungalow colony in Hurleyville, New York. But all forms of entertainment change and as soon as nightclubs, hotel work and television variety shows dried up, most entertainers went down to the sea in ships.

Through the 1980s, '90s and into the new century, the money and accommodations improved to the point that now the job is considered respectable, though the audiences are perhaps not as show-wise as they used to be.

But all of us "acts," especially me, need the bread, and where else can music acts, comics, joke tellers (not stand-ups, they get sitcoms and make millions), jugglers, singers of standards and ventriloquists that move their lips work? Unless they are under the age of thirty, then they might have a chance in pop music or Cirque du Soleil. Otherwise, the acts wind up on cruise ships if they are decent and I've seen thousands of acts and most of them are wonderful.

I am one of those acts. I am Ian Finkel, the World's Greatest Xylophonist. No one plays the xylophone better than I do. And I'm cute. Everybody says so. But concerts dried up, no one uses the xylophone much anymore and so I had to add "entertainment value" to my already virtuosic performances.

But here is the bad part. Getting to the ships is a different story. Travel at this time is a nightmare, especially if you have lots of luggage. And the ports of call are as ridiculous as they were in the days of Mark Twain when he traveled around the globe.

I became an "act" in the mid-1980s and I wound up on ships around 1993. Now, I am the "World's Greatest Xylophonist" (that's how I'm billed) and I do a wild evening of jazz, Latin and classical selections. I'm funny and delectably charming. I wear shiny purple and silver suits (I have a guy polish them before I leave town for each engagement) and where the hell else am I gonna work?!!

(Note to all those booking agents who don't use me: "You are just jealous of my talent!")

So here are a few stories of what I go through, what I've seen and what I view as my one-way-conversation with the world.

P.S. If my agent (who I love) reads this book . . . well . . . ah . . . Anything happening? I'm open from April to August.

"The world is a book and those who do not travel, read only a page." – Saint Augustine

"Well, then, I guess I wish I were illiterate." – Ian Finkel

The Hub of SHOWBIZ
(Cartagena, Columbia)

I judge a country by three things, the food, which includes the coffee, their music, the more brass the better, and how much cheap make-up and perfume the women wear. I'm partial to green eye shadow and coconut scents. But wait! There is a fourth category. The cigars.

If a country scores high in all four areas, I immediately fall in love with the place and want to live there forever, especially if it also has hot weather. The politics? Who cares? The educational system? Transportation? Oh, c'mon. I'm an entertainer, for God's sake!

But, as Ray Charles said in his version of *America, the Beautiful*, "Now, wait a minute!" I am an American entertainer and I wouldn't leave this country even if you told me that you were going to turn the Louvre into my private funhouse.

When you mention the city of Cartagena (you don't have to add Columbia), all the musicians and entertainers freeze in their tracks. For some unexplained reason, the cruise ship lines love to fly their "stars" to Cartagena to join a ship. Why not any other place in that area of the world? Who knows, but I have been there at least twenty-five times and each time I hate it all the more. Now, mind you, Columbia does score high in the above four areas. But to get in the stupid place is a nightmare of epic proportions, a battle royal that you cannot possibly win.

All entertainers sit on the plane, wringing their hands in prayer that when they arrive, wherever it is, their luggage will be there. And my bags are more important to me than the transportation of lifesaving body parts.

The two prominent airlines to Cartagena are Avianca, from Miami direct, or Copa (the airline of Panama), in which you make a stop in Panama City. Both lose luggage like the drug-toting bandits they are and it is a miracle to see your stuff on the smallish dirty conveyor belt when you get there.

When I was sent to Cartagena the first time, the "miracle" happened and all my luggage was there, wet from the humidity, but there. Five locals appeared out of nowhere smoothly chanting, "Senor, Senor, we help you?" and they grab your bags and brutally drag them to the guards near the exit door. Then, they each demand a few dollars apiece. All guards in Columbia have un-holstered firearms and, brother and sister, all you can do is smile and let them have their way with your stuff.

I've got five big bags and a carry-on (please look at picture on page 131): A large coffin-like case for the frame of the xylophone, sometimes I feel like Dracula traveling with his own coffin (except he wears black and I travel wearing orange), a case for the keyboard, one for the resonator tubes, a music case of fifty orchestrations and the large, normal suitcase of clothes, stage suits, sundries and humidor of cigars. The carry-on has my mallets, some emergency cigars and a few personal items. Oh, and a pocket trumpet, that's a regular trumpet rolled up so it's a bit smaller. I had a choice to buy a computer or a trumpet. Since I still write music with a quill, I chose the trumpet. It's sad that a Xylophonist needs to calm down by blowing a trumpet.

Round one:
The five guys named "Hector" drag the bags to the Uzi Immigration and Custom boys. The Uzis tell me to open everything up.

"Everything?"

"Si! Yes! Everything!"

And so I obey.

I'll continue in English, but it is mostly Spanish that is spoken and my vocabulary in that language is merely, gracias, banos, manana and cerveza por favor (even though I don't drink, but it sounds good).

"What is this?" I am asked.

"It's a xylophone."

"What?!"

"A xylophone . . . music . . . I am entertainer . . . a musician . . . I play on the ship."

They pull out the keyboard. They drop the resonators on the floor.

"Hey!" I cry.

"Do not speak, please. You have instruments? You sell them here in Columbia?"

"No, no, I'm going to the ship. I'm working on it. I...I..."

They pull out my trumpet.

"You sell this here in Columbia?"

"No, I work on the ship."

"You play it, Senor?"

"Yes, Si! I do!"

"You don't lie to us, Senor?"

"No way, please I. . .."

"Prove you play!!"

Uzi boy, numero uno, hands me the trumpet. I lick my lips. I stick the mouthpiece in. Uzi boys two and three run their hands through my clothes, rolling and kneading every suit and shirt into a jellyroll.

"Play! Play, Senor!"

So I put the horn to my lips and, without a decent warm-up, I play them an old Columbian melody, up and down the scales I go, nice intonation, pure sound. I finish off with a beautiful flourish. They all burst out with laughter and the five Hectors turn away. I should have tipped them more than as buck a piece.

"You stink, Senor! You must be for the Americanos! You may go!"

I look at them and am about to say, "Big deal! South of the border music critics," but I see their index fingers move to the triggers, so I just bow humbly and say, "Muchas gracias."

Round two:

I badly repack the cases, it takes twenty minutes (though to properly pack everything takes over two hours) and I am brought to a waiting van outside. The driver is from the local company that is supposed to "whisk" the entertainers through the mess I've just enjoyed. He throws all the luggage in the van and we pull away. Ten minutes later, we are at the port. He announces to me, "Customs and Immigration!"

Isn't that what I just did? I can see the ship; it is about fifty feet away. He directs me to a large stone table about ten feet long and tells me to put all my luggage on it and open it up.

"But, this is outdoors," I say. He shrugs and leaves. I haul all the bags up on to the stone table and a guard comes out.

Good grief, he hasn't washed since Juan Valdez's Bar Mitzvah. Did he just come from a road job? Nevertheless, I open every bag I've got. As I catch my breath, he thrusts his dirty hands into my music case and pulls out the lead alto sax book. He opens it and removes the second number from the book, "The Flight of the Bumble Bee Rhumba." The guard pulls the music close to his nose and smells the pages. This, I've never seen before. Usually people just say that my music smells.

"Excuse me, Senor Capitain, but, if I may ask, what are you doing?" I inquire. Without a smile, he answers, "Druggas, Senor."

I want to tell him why in hell would anyone bring drugs into Columbia a la coals to New Castle, but instead I go for the joke and say, "Then why don't you smell the tenor sax book? Those cats are all strung out and ..."

"Silencio, Senor!" he commands.

"Si," I sputter.

The guard rubs his face and replaces the music. He surveys everything and then dives into my suitcase, ripping out the gold silk shirt that I wear with the purple suit. Then he finds his treasure. It is a bottle of Vitamin Shop $12.95 multivitamins. He opens the bottle and pours the fat blue pills out on his hand. Then, here comes the nose! He inhales deeply.

I politely ask, "Druggas?"

"Silencio, Senor!" he commands.

Then, the primitive, open-holstered, son of a bitch tries to pour them back into the bottle. I wish I had his gun. Instead, I offer a gift.

"You may keep those, officer. They work wonders!"

He ignores me and puts the tablets back in the bottle. Later, I'll throw them away. The guard makes what I think are some mental notes about me, but then motions me to close everything up. I do this and the driver reappears. Once again, he savagely throws my bags into the van. I get in and we drive the fifty feet to the gangway of the ship.

Round three:

I just want to get the hell out of Cartagena, but now it's show time. The driver says, "Open everything."

"Where?" I cry. "On the ground?!!"

"Si, Senor."

So, on the filthy dock, I open up everything and here they come. Three guards, Uzis at the ready and four, not three mind you, big ugly dogs, mixed Columbian-Rhodesian Ridgeback Pit-bull Labs. The dogs jump on all my stuff and disgustingly nuzzle my xylophone. The first guard sees something in the large case. It is a black Hefty bag that is sandwiched in.

"What is this, Senor?" he asks.

"It is a bag of confetti," I solemnly answer. (I use the confetti in the finale of my show, it guarantees a standing ovation.)

"Que es? Con-fet-ti? Senor?"

"Yes. You know, confetti. I'm a xylo – no, I mean a clown."

"Clown?"

"Yes, Si!" I answer, then I do a little clown dance as I sing the "Stars and Stripes Forever" in la-de-dum syllables. Well, I can't do the lyrics in Spanish.

The dogs freeze and snarl, two guards lift their Uzis. I step back and stand at attention. The first guard thrusts his hand into the Hefty bag and pulls out a fistful of confetti. He holds it up to the sun and opens his hand. The paper bits go flying to the wind. He repeats this. Again, the stuff goes flying. Then, he pulls out a medium-large pocketknife, opens up the blade and stabs the bag.

It's New Year's Eve on the Cartagena Dock. Some people on the upper decks of the ship above us are looking down and see the blizzard of confetti and applaud. I bow to them. The guards mutter something in Spanish and the dogs go to their sides. The driver appears and says, "Okay, Senor, you may go!" I pack up everything and haul it all onto the ship.

I am met by the Cruise Director, a pink jacket, wearing a jet black toupee. I look at him and say, "Did you see all that?" He smiles the triumph of the Euro-trash and says, "Welcome, you're on tonight. Rehearsal in thirty minutes!"

The ship begins to pull away and I run to the rail of the open deck. I wave bye-bye to the Columbian guards and their dogs.

"The extreme pleasure we take in speaking of ourselves should make us apprehensive that it gives hardly any to those who listen to us." – La Rochefoucauld

"If you want to make it big as a performer, ignore that guy La Rochefoucauld." – Ian Finkel

This page has been left blank to give me time to get a sandwich, 3 espressos and a fresh cigar.

Me

I am a xylophonist. Oh, you don't know what that is? And you've never heard of me? Do you live in a log cabin?

Most people I know do not want to hear about my travels, or opinions, or anything I have to say. I've been called a chronic complainer, a blowhard, a sleezeball, you name it. I used to think they were jealous of my life, my talent, my cuteness, and I was probably right. So, now, I basically talk to no one (except Marty, I'll tell you about him later) except when I'm on the stage and then it's to the audience, which is not a singular cell like an amoeba, but, rather, a large fire-breathing, "make-me-laugh" dragon.

The other day, I forgot myself and endeavored to initiate a conversation with my daughter, Dara Gwynne, who is a brilliant young lady of twenty-five, well schooled, sensitive, gorgeous and a real New Yorker. I began with, "Do you know that there are places in the world, even in the United States, that when you buy a soda they don't have any straws?"

"God forbid!" she cried and walked out of the room. So much for conversation.

But that says it all about New York, we expect extras with everything: free baskets of rolls in the restaurants, free tastes of ice cream, pate, sausage, anything to taste while shopping. Free! We want free stuff. And we get it. We've always gotten it.

I was born in Brooklyn in 1948. During the 1950s you could go into any shop and the owner would give you a taste of something to get you going, to get you to buy. Smoked fish to chocolate-covered jelly candy. I basically wasted my teenage years going from store to store getting samples. I did start music when I was around fourteen, but I wasn't very serious. I took up the drums and I must admit I was lousy. I switched to trumpet when I was around sixteen and was worse. Maybe I thought that music would just come to me. Like a free sample. Well, it didn't and when I turned nineteen my music teacher informed me that I was much better suited to cleaning the men's room at the Astor Hotel, which he had already set up for me. I begged for one last chance. My teacher said it was too late to start the violin or piano.

"You're nineteen, kid! The free samples are all gone."

"But I don't want to clean toilets!"

"It's honorable woik."

"But, but. . ."

"Or you can get ya hack license and drive a cab, the city's easy!"

"But I hate driving."

"Okay, look here, drums, forget it, trumpet don't even think about it. I tell you what, you obviously love music, even though you don't work hard, so why don't you try something like, uh. . .xylophone?"

My teacher had one. I got behind it and picked up the mallets. The xylophone has the same keyboard as a piano, only forty-four keys. A piano has eighty-eight, so I'm half the man a good pianist is. I could read music from playing the trumpet and played the thing a bit.

Then, it hit me. I actually thought that playing the xylophone would get me girls. I'd be different, I'd be popular, I'd be oh so cute.

WRONG!

Someone, including my teacher, should have whispered in my ear,

"You want girls, you want cute, play guitar, dummo, not the xylophone."

But it didn't matter. I was hooked and quickly became addicted. From my nineteenth birthday until I was twenty-six, I practiced eight hours a day. And from twenty-six until now (I'm fifty-six), I average three to five hours a day, with no days off. I am proud to say that in all those years I may have missed no more than two weeks in total, which includes hospital stays (I'd leave early to go home and practice).

I was married at the age of twenty and a half and on my honeymoon night I made my new bride wait three hours until I was finished practicing. She never forgave me.

In music it is what you put in, put in big (and consistent), get out big. Maybe not career-wise, but artistically. There are no free anythings. I put in plenty.

The xylophone is a big instrument (see photo) and its history is a long one. There are arguments put up by scholars, none of whom who have actually played the thing, that it originated in Africa, wooden bars across gourds, or in South America, the marimba of Guatemala, or Asia, as in all gamelongs, or even in early Europe, where there were Renaissance instruments called the straw fiddle, which were bars of wood strung across straw. Most of this xylophone history means very little to me as I play an American xylophone, made in the USA. All my instruments are made in the USA.

I have two main xylophones. The first one was made in 1927 (the heyday of the instrument) and the second was made in the 1990s (fifty-some-odd years after the heyday of the instrument).

You do scales, arpeggios, all kinds of music on it, as on any other instrument, and if you are lucky (which you won't be), you'll get good in about fifty to sixty years as on any other instrument. No work, but you'll be good.

In the 1920s up to the 1950s, most people from all walks of life knew what a xylophone was. Now, they do not.

On one of my first jobs in the 1970s (it was a wedding), a man came up to me and said, "Hey, man, can you play a waltz on that thing?" I answered, "Of course." And I enthusiastically went into a medley of Strauss waltzes. Of course, the rest of the band knew them and when we had finished the waltz medley, the man came back up to the bandstand and said, "Gee, that was great. I didn't think you could play a waltz on that. . .ah. . .trampoline." I wasn't insulted. Not at all! Many musicians call it the vibes or marimba, stupid idiots and shame on them. I don't go up to a trumpet player and say, "Gee, what a shiny bugle you got."

I must tell you that my 1927 xylophone has a keyboard made of a species of Honduras Rose Wood that is extinct. In those days of handmade musical instruments they took the finest woods, cured and dried the stuff for years, and then made the instrument. Sadly, they didn't replant, so many fine old woods are gone. Same as comedy in Holland. They used it up in the beginning of the twentieth century and did not replant. Hence, since 1910 or so, there is no comedy in the Netherlands.

Now the instrument makers cut down a tree and make a xylophone. Or use a type of fiberglass instead of wood to make the keyboard. The new-age stuff approximates the sound of wood, as artificial strawberry flavor created in New Jersey laboratories, substitute for the real thing.

Now, I never "got girls" or any other free human samples, but I play the xylophone every day as if my life depends on it, which it surely does, not in the financial sense, but if I don't play, I am nothing.

A Home Boy in Dakar, Senegal

In this age, being the world's greatest xylophonist is akin to being the guy who owns the biggest collection of 78s or one who can brush his teeth the fastest or hold his breath the longest, etc. Who cares? Not many. But old-time vaudeville acts such as myself, though I feel fresh and new, in this new age of showbiz, need all the publicity (which leads to gigs) as we can get.

    I was sitting home, it was about two in the afternoon and I was lighting up my breakfast cigar. The telephone rang and I absentmindedly answered it. Usually, I let the answering machine take it so I could study the message and call back later. I picked up the call and it was a guy from a major music keyboard magazine (I'll call him Fredtzel) and he told me that since I am the world's greatest exponent of the xylophone, he wanted to do an article about me. I flipped out and immediately went into my spiel that I could play anything, I'm a great sight-reader, I orchestrate, I smoke five cigars a day and drink eight cups of espresso by dinnertime. Fredtzel cut in and said, "That's all fine, but I have a much better idea for the article. I want to compare you to the xylophonists of Senegal. After all, World Music is the thing and I think it would be neat to compare what you do to what they do."

I could feel the black bile traveling up my esophagus. I love all kinds of music, but just what in hell does Fredtzel think!?! You wouldn't compare Jascha Heifetz to a one-string washtub player. And he said the word "neat."

Gently, I cut in: "ARE YOU NUTS? Look here, Fredtzel; those Senegalese xylophonists play a primitive instrument, two inches from the floor, with mallets topped with water buffalo dung. They live in mud huts. They play by ear. They. . ."

"But it would be sweet to. . ."

"Sweet? Neat?" I snarled. "I popped out of my momma wearing a tuxedo, I had a cigar in my mouth, and it was lit. I read, R-E-A-D music. I've played with the New York Philharmonic Orchestra, the Met Opera House Orchestra, films, radio, television. Why, I even had coffee once with Vanilla Ice! How can you compare me with those guys! It's like comparing a stickball player with Babe Ruth! Now, listen here! Hello? Hello? Hello? Hell!"

He had already hung up. God, I felt good letting him have it so early in the day. I hung up the phone and it immediately rang. I picked it up.

"I also wrote arrangements for Regis Philbin!" I scream.

"Ian? What are you talking about? This is your agent, Melinda. I just called to offer you a job on a cruise ship in the Mediterranean."

"Oh," I answered, sotto voce, "Sorry, Melinda, I'll take it. When is it?"

"Today's Friday. You leave Monday."

Monday, I was on the plane to Barcelona, Spain. By Tuesday, I realized that the ship was through with the Mediterranean and was on its way down the coast of Africa. Two days later, I did my show. Another day and we stopped at Dakar, Senegal.

This was a God-awful place. You can't go anywhere unaccompanied. If you do, you die! So, you get off the ship and just stroll up and down the dock, which is actually marvelous. Vendors of all kinds selling carvings (lots of giraffes) and thousands of leather bags of all sizes. Well, here I was, if just for a few hours, so I wouldn't be able to hear any Senegalese xylophone players who are my peers. But perhaps I could pick up a few gifts for myself.

So I looked at the leather bags. Now, I know these fellas like to bargain, so after I find a bag, a smallish one, good for carrying cigars and smoking paraphernalia, I asked the vendor, "How much?"

"One hundred and eighty-five dollars, U.S." was his reply.

I gave him the look of the "Brooklyn Consumer" and said, "Sorry, no thanks."

"Wait, my friend, for you it is fifty dollars."

"Fifty?"

"Ah, no, my friend, make me any offer."

I eyeball him and say, "What kind of leather is this?"

"The very best gazelle."

"Oh, and I wanted something in leopard. Okay, I'll give you twenty."

"Sold, my friend."

I gave him the money and felt a tap on my shoulder. It was one of a group of guests from the ship, a big Texan with a loud ten-gallon hat.

"Mr. Finkel, y'all should go down the other end. They are selling what y'all play!"

"You mean he's got a Musser #50 made in Chicago, full-size American, extended-range custom-made xylophone?"

"Ha, ha, no, one of them little African thangs. C'mon, boy, go with us and give us a tune on it."

As we walked down the pier, I told them how the magazine wanted to do an article comparing me to the very guy we were going to see. Of course, they didn't get it, but we reached the other end of the dock and there was my man. Tall, about six-seven, wearing the traditional African dashiki, with lots of beads - goodness, he was shinier than I am - and a beard down to his middle. On the ground was the instrument; raw wood, gourds for resonators and cheap hemp-like rope holding the thing together. A piece of junk. But I respect everyone and their music, so I approached the man and looked all the way up to him and said, "My, my, my. . .a xylophone, I think. May I try it?"

The Texan and group stifled their laughter; they know what's coming.

"You may," answered my African twin in a beautiful James Earl Jones voice.

"Oh. . .but before I do. . .may I inquire how much is this fine instrument?" I politely asked.

"One hundred and fifty, US," came the answer from above.

"Ah, yes, thank you, I will give it a spin," I said as I get down on all fours to try it, and getting down on all fours is not a specialty of mine. I figured the man would see that I was a homeboy, a xylophonist, and, of course, lower the price. I positioned myself on my haunches and picked up the two dung-topped mallets. I stared at the thing and then. . .I took off like the God of Xylo that I am, up and down the thing I go, faster and faster, scales, arpeggios, double notes, flashy rhythms, an Italian song, a Jewish Freilach. I finished off with a fugue of an old Senegalese folk song. Oh, I was so darn clever, and by this time the thirty or forty people that had assembled around me burst into tumultuous applause. I looked up at Mr. Senegal and in a coarse sneer he said, "You are professional. For you, it is two hundred dollars!"

A Home Boy in Dakar, Senegal

"That which probably hears more stupidities than anything else in the world is a painting in a museum."
— Edmond and Jules De Goncourt

"Thank you for using the word probably. In truth, what a xylophonist hears after he plays, tops 'em all." — Ian Finkel

This page has been left blank so the reader can "smoke 'em if you got 'em.

The Bells of Saint Petersburg, Russia

If you were brought up in Brooklyn, New York, as I was, you think you are a tough guy. Done everything, seen everything, nothing scares you, unless you are Jewish. If you are Jewish, that means you have a Jewish mother and she'll put the fear of the world in you as easy as ordering take-out.

"Don't do that, don't eat that, don't wear that, don't look at that, and don't think that. I suppose all *that* makes them great mothers, but you do grow up being their baby prince forever.

My mother is a pro. She'll debate you on any topic and not give up until she wins, even if it takes years. My mother (and father) still calls me every day and the phone call is a maddening replay of parent-to-child conversation. It takes place always at eleven p.m.

Mother: Is everything okay?
Jewish Son (me): Everything is fine.
Mother: Something's wrong, I can feel it.
Jewish Son: Nothing's wrong.

Mother:	How's the family?
Jewish Son:	Everyone is fine.
Mother:	Are they all home?
Jewish Son:	No.
Mother:	Where are they?
Jewish Son:	Out...working. Wherever.
Mother:	Why aren't the children in bed?
Jewish Son:	Well, you may recall that my son is married, has children of his own and lives upstate.
Mother:	And your daughter, the pearl of my life? She's too young to be out at this hour.
Jewish Son:	She's twenty-five, Ma! She works at night, has a car, votes and....
Mother:	The door locked?
Jewish Son:	Yes.
Mother:	Is the gas off?
Jewish Son:	I switched to electric ten years ago!
Mother:	You're not leaving town again, are you?
Jewish Son:	Yes, I am.
Mother:	Where are you off to now?
Jewish Son:	Russia.
Mother:	Gevalt!! Oi Vey!! Are you crazy? How can you go there?
Jewish Son:	Well, I told my landlord I'm a genius and the dirty rat still wants his rent. Can you imagine that?
Mother:	Are you going on a ship?
Jewish Son:	Yes.
Mother:	Stay away from the rail; you'll fall off, into the water. And don't get off of the ship. If you tell anyone who you are, YOU – WILL – BE – KIDNAPPED!
Jewish Son:	Ma, I'm fifty-six years old.

Mother:	So? Nu?
Jewish Son:	Put Dad on.
My Father:	Who else is in the show with you?
Jewish Son:	Well, it's me on xylophone, there's a magician, a juggler act and a dance team.
My Father:	Ha! A week of opening acts!

But I was thrilled to be sent to a ship that was cruising the Baltic. It was to stop for two days in St. Petersburg, Russia. One of the great cities of the world for music, St. Petersburg gave musical birth to Tchaikovsky, Rimsky-Korsakov, Borodin, et al, and the famous Hermitage Museum, which has rows and rows of Rembrandt to Picasso. And to think that on my fifth Chanukah I got a paint-by-numbers set.

Just before going to pick up the ship in Copenhagen, my old pal Marty gave me a compilation book of Mark Twain's writings entitled *The Travels of Mark Twain*. (Marty is a fabulous drummer and has played everywhere for everyone and not only is my best pal, he constantly reminds me that I am the World's Greatest Xylophonist. Although he does not smoke cigars, he is still a fine American man.) Twain commented on the lack of hygiene in Russia, how the men smell, and Marty reminded me that though the music is great, "Finkel, you'd better bring your cigars and don't expect to find too many ladies with cheap make-up."

"But Russia used to deal with Cuba. I'll get my fill of Cohibas and..."

"No, you won't," added Marty. "They'll still be expensive ... and hard to get ... plus, I hear the food stinks ... and they hate Jews ... and you'll hate them." Marty and I are old-time ghetto-style Jews. We speak Yiddish to each other when we don't want the other musicians to understand and we eat at the Second Avenue Deli.

Four days later, I pulled into St. Petersburg. Mother Russia. All the entertainers are issued a "Blue Card," which means you work on the ship. Don't lose it or it'll cost you $150 and remember to take your passport everywhere. An elderly British comic grabbed me before I got off of the ship and said, "Be careful, old boy, and after the Hermitage go to the Freaks."

"Freaks?"

"Yes, an old Tsar owned it and there are jars of human deformities within. Loads of fun, what!?"

I caught a cab and went to the Hermitage. I was not prepared mentally for such a place. I headed straight for the Rembrandts. I became dizzy at the rows and rows of perfect masterpieces. Where does one stand at first? It shook me to the core. I steadied myself and made a choice. I was four feet from "The Return of the Prodigal Son." Slowly, the painting drew me in, not the details, not the shadings of color nor the basic composition. It was the feeling I got from the images. My soul began to connect to this wonder and I stood there humbly as an artist should. I admit that I began to weep and as not to be publicly embarrassed, I tried to cover my tears. My body was still yet my soul was moved. As I tried to pull some air into my lungs, a tour group from one of the many ships formed their hideous clump in front of me.

The Russian guide announced, "People, we must not look at this work for more than a moment as it is not very important and we must move on. Quickly, now, three buses are waiting, heh, heh, and there is the Tsarina's golden carriage that was used in the cinema to see!"

My artistic moment was ruined. The act of my soul being dashed upon the rocks shook me to the very marrow of my bones. Oh, they'll get a show from me! Are they the "Freaks" I was told to see?

Yeah, sure, uh huh. They are the Freaks. But after the Hermitage and its rows and rows of Rembrandts they say they acquired (stole), I do go to the Freaks. What can top rows and rows of any great master? Freaks! A Museum of Freaks! Which is a poor term to use. The place was mobbed. Layers of people pushing each other to see the three-headed blah, blah or the half-something. Half? Oh, dear Lord. And most of the men, especially those in military uniform, did smell.

But I got around the city. I figured it out right away that all you had to do was plan the day out so you basically circled the one hotel that had the only clean men's room. So you cab it and come back, use the facilities and go somewhere else, up and back. Cabs are cheap and for $3 U.S., I went to the famed cemetery. In one area alone there was all the old boys, Tchaikovsky, Rimsky-Korsakov, Borodin, Glinka etc., all buried near each other with beautiful tombstones. All I could think of saying was, "Hello, boys, I know you're waiting for me... See ya soon."

I cabbed it back to the ship for dinner, but first stopped at the Nevsky Prospekt, a huge street, and find the music store that sold old violin music, which I collect, cheap and great. But I noticed something. There are lots of police (or, shall I say, James Bond movie extras) stopping suckers, I mean tourists, for jaywalking and letting them go for cash. Another scam. I must point out that in this town they've got many types of police - blue shirts, black shirts, grey shirts - all dirty and smelly and mean and most definitely corrupt, to say the least.

After dinner on the ship, I invited the whole band, who had the night off, to go out with me into town for drinks. The piano player, a lovely British fellow, who I've heard recently became a monk or priest or something holy, told me there was a shuttle bus that would take us into town to the Hollywood Disco-Casino and we could get a drink there. Fine. And off we went, your faithful xylophone virtuoso and eight cats from the band. We went through the gate and got on the shuttle, which was a large bus. I hate buses, all musicians do, but it was free. On the bus was another band from a ship that was docked further down and I know them, so I invited one and all to go out with me. After all, an American xylophone virtuoso could certainly afford at least twenty drinks, if he is working, and, most likely, I'm the only one.

The ride was short and we got to the Hollywood. What a dump, huge, dirty, hundreds of hookers all dressed like Cyndi ("Girls Just Want to Have Fun") Lauper, but with the wrong make-up on, no cigars and definitely no espresso.

The Russian Disco music was blaring and there was three big, four-hundred-pound, hairy guys on stage having a beer-drinking and banana-eating contest. Disgusting. I cut through the wall of hookers and get a waitress at the bar. She comes over and takes the order for the twenty or so drinks. The bill came to twelve dollars and fifty cents and I gave the waitress a fiver as a tip. (Things are cheap there; not the hookers, they want two hundred and fifty. I asked just for laughs.)

Ten minutes later, I easily tired of the bad show and the twenty-seventh chorus of "The Song of the Volga Boatmen" in a Donna Summer Disco beat and said to a few of the guys that we should get out of here and find a place for coffee and cake. (How Jewish of me.) Four guys say okay and we left. I hope that those who remained had the two-fifty. I must point out that I am not a rowdy person and the five of us were sober and walking up the street quietly and very respectfully.

Out of the sewers come about a dozen grey shirts, Russian cops. They grab us brutally and three of them dragged me into an unmarked van. But I kept my composure. In the van there was a table and smallish chairs. They sat me down. I was facing two of the s.o.b.s and the third, a Russian bear of a man, who reminded me of Piatigorsky, the great Russian cellist, sat with his back to the side door. The ceiling was four inches above our heads.

"What is this?" I asked. "I haven't done anything."

Grey shirt number one, who is across from me, says, "Empty pockets, now!"

I do as he says and put my wallet and passport on the little table. The three cops go thru my wallet separating the cash ($80 or so), the credit cards, receipts and photos of my beloved xylophone that I carry with me. The passport and the $150 blue card are also there.

Grey shirt number two says, "Empty pockets!!"

"But I just did. That's everything."

The Russian bear put his ham-sized hand on my shoulder and gave it a squeeze. It is vise-like and hurt like all hell. I guess he doesn't play the cello. But I was, shall we say, "cool."

In a bass trombone growl, he barked, "You have drugs?"

I looked at him insanely and answered, "No, of course, not! I'm a musician (that was a stupid thing to say) and work on the ship!"

"Your comrades have drugs?" Shirt number one added.

"What? No...wait...I mean...I don't know. Look, fellas...I mean officers, I'm just out with the boys for something to eat and we weren't doing anything."

I looked out the window and see the four musicians. They have been released. Obviously, I was fingered by the Hollywood. I'm the American with the cash! I knew these Rooskie-Commie cops were gonna be rough and tough.

I looked at the bear. He turned in his seat and gave the other two grey shirts a look. In beautiful synchronization, they all pulled out short rubber hoses. They stared deeply at me.

"Wait a minute, please!" I said. "Just the face, not the hands!"

"If we keep you, it is three days before a phone call," the bear said, "and we could..."

I interrupted and said, "Look, just take the wallet and the cards and the blue card and the cash and everything and just give me my passport and..."

"Stand up," my Russian bear instructed.

"How can I stand, the ceiling is four inches above and..."

"Stand now!" my lover roared. So I managed to half stand and my bear lover reached over and frisked me - and I mean *deep*. Brutally, he went into my pants and messed around. He grabbed my "bells" and rang them to that old Rachmaninoff tune that all pianists play, "The Bells of Moscow." My "ice" began to thaw.

"Now you sit."

I sat down. The first thing that crossed my mind is that the Rooskie-Commie Bastard had his way with me and didn't even kiss me or buy me dinner. Grey shirt number one put everything in his pocket, but gave me back the passport. My lover then opens the side door behind him, grabs my shirt and pulls while saying, "Now, you go."

And he threw me out into the gutter and I instinctively covered my face with my hands and rolled three or four times and came to a heap on the ground. My Max Factor cover-up was smeared and my silk lime-green shirt was torn. Yes, I'm a Metrosexual. The van pulled away.

When I saw that they were a block down the street, I called out to the four musicians who were running toward me.

"I kicked their asses! Let's go back to the ship for coffee and cake."

We grabbed a cab and returned to the ship. All I could think of was that my mother was soooo-right. Back on the ship, I avoided the outside railings, went to my cabin and locked the door.

All Roads Lead to Rome, Italy

But first a word about Venice, a brief note about San Marco Square. When I first got there, I had such high hopes for the place. Okay, the food in Italy is great, except for pizza, which is much better in New York. In fact, it is an American thing, isn't it? And the people are basically very attractive, though I did have to go to many of the churches, couldn't find a synagogue, and pray that none of the women would raise their arms and yell "taxi." Lady Gillette has not arrived yet. What I want to touch upon is that in San Marco Square they have various bands playing and on first sight you think you're going to hear a great authentic rendition of "La Gazza Ladra" or "La Fortza del Destino" (the overtures). After all, most of the bands are made up of a clarinet, accordion, two violins, cello, bass and piano. But, instead, what you hear is either the theme from *The Godfather* or some horrible Andrew Lloyd Webber tune complete with the wrong chords. It proves my point that music has turned downward all around the world. Well, the hell with it. But, then, every church in Italy is a museum; so enjoy the paintings they've got.

So, in Rome, I was walking with two musicians from the ship and we were going to eat. *Eat.* Italian Food. It's still the best and here we were in Italy, pasta-land. We spotted a place that looked good, not far from the Coliseum, but before we could cross the street to get to it, we were surrounded by an elderly woman, carrying a baby, followed by her three thousand children. Really, there were only six kids, but they circled us like Custer at the last stand. They begged for money and, being the world's most benevolent xylophonist, I was about to give her some, but I remembered a training film I saw on the ship a few nights earlier that showed how the mother has a false arm, which is carrying the baby, and picks your pocket with her concealed arm as you dole out the cash. Sure enough, as she drew close with the baby (which, if you looked close, was actually a baby-doll), she stuck her hand in my pocket. Well, guess what? I never carry stuff there anymore when I travel. All my cash is in a pouch inside my pants, which is held there by a second belt of kangaroo-skin. Poetic justice. So, all she got was practice. I yelled, "Get away from me, you Gypsy hag!" but one of her kids, a small boy, jumped up and pulled two Dominican cigars from my breast pocket and took off. One of the musicians, Jack, a trombone player, reacted quickly and ran after the thief. The rest of the children scattered and Mama, with the fake baby, sprinted away like Seabiscuit at Belmont. I followed suit, but my top speed was four miles an hour and I only get a quarter of a mile to the gallon of espresso.

Jack caught the little kid three blocks away and, what seemed like an hour and a half later, I finally got there. He held him for me and the poor boy forked over my stogies. I removed the wrapper from one and lit up, passed it over to the kid and said, "Smoke it, Sonny." And the little varmint did! He drew in deep and blew a big blue cloud into Jack's face. I screamed with laughter.

"Man, this kid is tough!" I tell Jack and gave the boy five bucks US. Naturally, we let him go and headed back to the restaurant. The other musician, I forget his name, but I do remember that he was a lousy bass player, was already in there, halfway through his salad of buffalo mozzarella drizzled with pesto.

I'm Sittin' on Topkapi, Istanbul, Turkey

It's a shame that most of the cruise ships I appear on do not stop in Turkey anymore. It's a fascinating place, though a filthy one. The food is great, the Mosques are a thrill and the music is fascinating. They make the best cymbals in the world. It's where the Zildjian Company came from. Ask any drummer and he or she will wax on for hours about some old "Constantinople" cymbals he almost acquired. But the men there are nuts. Did you see the movie *Midnight Express*? See it. And no one washes their hands, I've seen that.

We pulled into Istanbul and I made a date with three ladies who worked on the ship. Two were lecturers on the Middle East and the third a lovely singer in the revue group on board. We met off the ship and walked down the dock where there were dozens of restaurants. As we walked, the lecturers went on about how awful the treatment of women is in the Middle East and the singer, who happened to be from Casablanca, totally agreed. I, of course, agreed as well. I don't care if the person in question is dog, cat or whatever, if they can play their instrument, they're in my band. Naturally, I'd prefer if they smoke cigars, but you can't have it all. (By the way. . .Vienna Philharmonic, drop dead! They are the only orchestra in the world to not allow women in it. What year is this?) Even as we walked together, the local guys leered at us and made remarks. Of course, I don't speak Turkish, but the two lecturers did and they translated. The basic drift of the comments made by the locals as they watched us go by was, "There is an American pimp and his three whores."

I'd answer back, "Go wash your hands!"

The ladies were dressed very modestly and I was in my usual dinner attire, powder-blue leisure suit, Panama hat and a fine eight-inch Nicaraguan Maduro in my mouth, unlit. Nothing weird with that.

Every restaurant had a guy in front trying to get people in. We stopped at each one and the lecturers inquired in Turkish as to what was on the menu. At the fifth place, the owner, at least I think that's who he was, stopped in mid-conversation with the ladies and stared at me. Tears of joy filled his eyes and he asked the ladies something in Turkish. They translated to me that he thought I was some American movie star he'd seen and he was offering up all kinds of food. I told them to tell the owner that I was who he thought I was and then some. It would insure us of a great meal. The singer turned to me and said, "What pictures were you in?"

"I was an extra in the movie *Independence Day*. How could you miss me?"

In we went and we were told not to order. The owner asked me for my autograph and I signed, "Robert De Niro."

I look nothing like Robert De Niro. I am much more appealing, kind of a cross between Pavarotti, Robert Redford and Golda Meir. But, perhaps, my wardrobe overshadowed my looks. And the cigar added a touch of Che to the whole thing.

Within seconds, all kinds of great food and weird, but also great, booze covered our table. Lively conversation took hold and we were having a hell of a time. After a while, I needed to use the men's room and I asked a waiter as to its location.

"Up the stairs and there it is."

I got up and went to the nearby stairway. At the bottom of the stairs was a young boy-man in apron and jalaba, about fourteen years old or so with amazing steel-grey eyes. He moved toward me and linked his arm under mine as to help me up the stairs. Okay, I'm not that old but "what the hell," up we went. Three steps from the top he went for it. The man-boy copped a feel, for cryin' out loud! I mean, he reached over and put his hand on my manhood and gave a squeeze!

Now, I was raised in a showbiz environment. I've been felt up by bigger stars than this kid. Most men would react in the American style, that is, to haul off and punch the kid down the stairs. Not me. I don't do that. Instead, I let out a "Whooo!" *La Cage Aux Folles* style, and smiled. I do the three more steps and went into the restroom. Finished, I returned to the stairs where my new lover was waiting in attendance. He linked up and helped me down the steps and three steps before we hit the bottom, he went for it again, and this time I gave off a bigger, louder, "Who Hoooo!!"

The whole restaurant looked up at me. My trio of ladies asked, "What was *that* all about?" And I answered, "He copped a feel! Twice!!"

I wish I could get a laugh like I received then when I'm on stage. The ladies screamed, adding, "Well, now you know how it feels, etc., etc."

"Oh yeah," I snapped back, "the laugh's on him. That kid thinks he just felt up Robert De Niro, but instead all he copped was an old xylophonist!"

The next day, I took a taxi to Topkapi, one of the great museums of the world if you want to see where concubines were kept. I don't, but they had a window of spoons that was a riot. The bottoms were of pearl, shells, glass, etc., and the handles made of various gold and silver, studded with jewels, mostly singles, so I could not figure out for the life of me how they did dinner. I mean, don't you need service for two hundred? I managed to push through the crowd who were staring at the famous baseball-size emerald on the handle of a scimitar. That was enough for me and I had to get back to the ship.

I found a taxi and asked the driver if I might sit in the front seat. He was delighted (a bit too much) and answered, "Yes, yes, my friend."

I told him I was going to the cruise ship terminal and he hit the pedal hard. As we drove, he asked me my name. "My friend, what is your name, my friend?"

"Ian Finkel, the world's greatest xylophonist, from America, and I smoke eight cigars a day and I drink twelve cups of espresso by lunch," I answer.

"My name is Elif Kadir."

He smiled, I smiled. As we flew through the streets of Istanbul, I suddenly felt something. The driver had his hand on my left leg and it was traveling north! I think, how far is this guy going to go? I couldn't haul off and belt him, he'd slam into a wall and we'd be killed. It was too early for a *La Cage Aux Folles* "whooo." So, I did the only thing a red-blooded American man could do. I put my hand on his leg and made like I was going to kiss him.

"Pull over, you fool!" I yelled and he came to a screeching stop. I hopped out and threw a fist of money through the window.

"Beat it, chump, or I'll kill ya!" I screamed and, shocked as to his loss, he took off. I got back to the ship, assembled the three ladies and recounted my story. Again, I got the big laugh, no sympathy whatsoever.

After they dried their tears of laughter, the singer said, "Finkel, you're pretty hot in Turkey. If only you could get an audience to like you as much."

"Everything can be borne except contempt." – Voltaire

"Ladies and Gentlemen, I thank you." – Ian Finkel

Getting Paid and "Negotiations"

Everyone is underpaid. I've always said that police officers and firemen should start out at two hundred and fifty thousand a year. Could you do what they do? No way.

I should be making twenty million a year. Could you do what I do? Would you want to? I am grotesquely underpaid. All good musicians are. You seem to get good money for a gig then you are out of work for six months and the money runs out fast. What with instruments, sheet music, cigars, cologne, shiny suits, the dough quickly disappears.

Every cruise ship act I have ever met has the same story about being paid on board a ship. Usually the money is sent to your agent, the ten percent deducted and you get the balance sent to your house. Once in a while you are paid on board and each and every act goes through this: You get on a long line at the Purser's office along with various other employees from all over the world. All of them except for you are getting slave wages. That's how cruise ships have existed. Hire from the vast pool of unemployed Indonesians, Indians from Goa, Eastern Europeans, etc. etc., pay them crap, work 'em to death and they'll say thank you for a fourteen-hour day, seven days a week, no days off for eight months. In their country, the money will go far. Not for an entertainer from the USA.

So here you are on line and you get your turn and the Purser counts out the hundreds, and, believe me, after three or four you'll already be getting more than an officer. But. . .it took you years to be able to do what you do. And you have invested a lifetime in study, instruments, costumes and you have to get up in front of an audience and tame the beast. So here is the dialogue we all have to go through:

PURSER:	(After counting out your fortune) You get all this money and you only work two shows one night in the week?!!
THE ACT:	Please, just give me my money so I can go.
PURSER:	You make as much as the Captain!!
THE ACT:	I don't think so.
PURSER:	I could do what you do!
THE ACT:	You can?
PURSER:	Yes!
THE ACT:	You can do an act for fifty-four minutes in front of an audience, playing an instrument that took thirty years to get down, talk to the crowd, try to be funny, get a standing ovation, rehearse the band, pay thousands for an instrument, thousands for musical arrangements, thousands for costumes. . .*and* be cute?
PURSER:	Well. . .ah. . .
THE ACT:	Please, recount my money, slowly.

At this point, the Purser turns red and recounts and gives you the look of death. After this scene, the word is out so you get bad room service and everyone on the staff gives you the cold shoulder.

Or you could have said to the Purser, "Oh, gee, that's great! Put your act together and get me your videotape and I'll send it to my agent."

They not only never do, but couldn't in a million years.

So I never do a ship that pays on board. Too embarrassing.

Here's How I "Negotiate"

I was called to do a show or write some music. The person calling me described the job as, "to do what is needed" and invited me to a meeting to discuss my fee and what I was going to do. I will use fictitious numbers to prove my point: I figured they had called ME, not just anyone but ME. The job involved performing and writing and should pay $100, but they called ME. They could easily have afforded to pay $150, but since they called ME, and since I have been out of work for six months, I'd take it for $89.

I went to the meeting. Around the table were three lawyers, two accountants and four other non-theatrical types that knew nothing about music or show business. I described my show and how I'd write the music, four trombones here. . .twenty violins there, drums, elephants, cocktails for two. They sat and listened a bit, made their silly suggestions and eventually it got down to the money. Before I said what it should pay, one of the lawyers offered me $15. "That low!" "Take it or leave it!" They waited for my answer. Lawyers and accountants love to negotiate. I don't play on their turf so I said nothing and slowly reached down into my briefcase and pulled out a mirror, the old-fashioned kind that ladies used to use when they did their hair. I looked into the mirror. I made cute faces into the mirror. I smiled into it, but I said nothing. This act took about two minutes. Try to sit still doing nothing for two minutes. It is an eternity. Eventually, beads of sweat began to form on one and all (not me) and one of the negotiators said, "What are you doing?!!!"

I answered, "I just want to see if I am as big a schmuck as you think I am." Then I put the mirror back in the briefcase, got up and headed for the door. If they really wanted me (they usually don't), they would stop me at the door and offer $68.

I then said, "Call me when you have $165."

You have to be prepared to "eat it" when they don't call. Or if they do it is usually $150, but you know they are never going to be satisfied with whatever you play or write.

> *"Travelers, like poets, are mostly an angry race."*
> – Sir Richard Burton

"And they all seem to come to my shows." – Ian Finkel

Dance of the Sugar PLUM
(Cape Town, South Africa)

The travel agents who book the flights for the cruise ship entertainers make plenty of mistakes. And wherever you are sent, a port agent is supposed to meet you and "whisk" you to the ship, or to a hotel if you are staying overnight in order to make a connection with the ship. Eight out of ten times those guys never show up and you could be stranded in an airport at two a.m. The place could be anywhere from Cape Verde to Bora Bora. You have to fend for yourself, find a taxi (good luck), find a hotel (ha, ha) or pray you won't be mugged - or worse.

I have had a four a.m. phone call from an entertainer crying the blues.

"Hello, Ian?"

"Yeah, who's this?"

"It's Jerry. I am in Punta Arenas."

"It's four a.m."

"There's no ship, nobody, nothing."

"How's the weather?" I ask.

"It's freezing!"

"That's because you're in Punta Arenas, Chile!"

"I know!"

"I'll bet," I add sympathetically. "They should have sent you to Puntarenas, Costa Rica!"

"How far away is that from where I am?"

I try not to cry along, but, sotto voce, I say, "Jerry, you are on the bottom of South America. You've got to get to the top and then some. The bastards sent you a million miles off! Fly home, have your agent get you reimbursed and the hell with them!"

"But I need the job, the money, I . . . I . . . I . . . I. . ."

At this point in my career, I have a way to teach the ship travel agents a lesson. First of all, I never go anywhere unless I check the destination out first. I travel only on direct flights, if possible, so as to give the airlines less of a chance to lose my luggage. But since a port agent might not show up when I arrive, here is a story with a fine example for all the entertainers to follow.

My brother Elliot (a concert pianist) and I were both booked for appearances on the famous *Cunard QE2*. We were to fly to Cape Town, South Africa, sleep overnight and get on the ship the next day. After a week or so, we would cross the Atlantic to Miami. It's a long flight and you have to switch in Johannesburg. The flights were fine and we got to Cape Town at ten p.m.

My brother travels with more suitcases than a Barbara Streisand World Tour, so between us there are fifteen pieces of luggage and two carry-ons, but, thanks to the Gods of travel, all the bags made it.

We collected our baggage and looked for the port agent. No one. The airport thinned out. We called our agent in New York and she gave us the name of the hotel and number of the port agent in Cape Town. We called him and he told us he hadn't worked for Cunard in three years, cheerio, pip pip and you are on your own. Now, I go into action. I found a guy lurking around the parking lot with a small safari-like vehicle. I offered him a hundred and he lit up. He loaded us up and took us to the hotel, a big beautiful high-rise. Our bags were brought in.

I stepped up to the desk and announced, "Finkel and Finkel here." The man behind the desk dove into his computer and then looked up and said, "You're not supposed to be here until tomorrow."

"What am I? Saran wrap? We're here now!"

"But, sir, we haven't any rooms."

"Well, we can't go around Cape Town looking for a place. Don't you have anything?"

He surveyed his computer. With an odd smile he said, "Well, sir, all I really have is the two bridal suites."

"Those are our rooms!"

"Well, each suite is three rooms, two bedrooms and a living room and two baths and. . ."

"And we'll take them both."

"Both, sir?"

"That's it and that's all, here's my credit card." I gave him the plastic. He looked at me and said, "That's six hundred U.S. per night, each."

And I said, "Till what time do you have room service?"

"Twenty-four hours, sir,"

All this time my brother had been silent. He took me aside and said, "Does your card cover all this?"

"Watch, listen, and learn." Ten minutes later, we are in our suites. I called him up and told him to come over. He did.

"Sit down and watch me punish the cruise line, port agent and half of South Africa for their stupid Apartheid crap." He sat. I went to the phone and called room service. A beautifully deep woman's voice answers.

"Room service. What is your pleasure?"

"How many jars of Macadamia nuts do you have?"

"Jars, sir? I have several cases of Macadamia nuts, sir."

"That's what I want. I love 'em."

"Cases, sir?"

"Yes. Two cases of Macadamias."

"There are twelve jars to a case."

"Naturally. And I want meat. What kind of meat is there?"

"Sir, we have the finest steaks in South Africa."

"Certainly. Then send up six with all the side dishes."

"How would you like them prepared, sir?"

I looked at my brother, we're Jewish, and Jews eat their meat well done, no blood, it's more than cultural. "Well done," I said, and my brother nodded his approval.

"And," I continued, "for starters, how about some appetizers, about a dozen plates, you know, local stuff. . .and four bottles of red wine (yes, I know that Jews don't drink), nothing but the best. And what have you got for dessert?"

"Well. . .well, sir. . .we have some very fine cake or perhaps you'd like an aged cheese. May I also suggest our delicious coffee?"

"You may. And some chocolates would top it off."

"Will that be all, sir?"

"Yes, and please, do your best to bring it as soon as possible as we have been traveling for many hours and we wish to dine before we retire."

"Yes, sir!"

I hung up and asked my brother if I had left anything out.

"Sparkling water," he said.

"Sorry!" I redialed and added a case of twelve bottles and six bottles of Dom Perignon, '64. I might want to bathe later.

An hour and some showbiz stories passed and the doorbell rang. I let them in, four waiters, stiff, regal, beautiful. They laid out the feast on the table in the center of my suite. One waiter started to open up a case of the Macadamia nuts.

"I'll do that and thank you, gentlemen. The bill, please." It's for eight hundred and twenty-five dollars and thirteen cents. (Actually, it is in South African rands, but that is the US rate.) Cheap! I signed the bill, giving them a hundred-dollar tip. They left with weird smiles.

Again, I looked at my stunned brother. "Do not speak," I say and, with great effect, I opened up the cases of nuts. I removed six jars and opened them. I spilled the contents of the half-dozen jars on the floor, as Fred Astaire would dust his dance floor with sand. Then I took off my clothes. And then I danced! I danced my world-famous ballet.

"This is entitled the Revenge of the Sugar Plum Xylophonist."

I sang be-bop syllables to Tchaikovsky's "Dance of the Sugar Plum Fairy," from the Nutcracker Suite, if you get my drift, and danced and danced and danced. When finished (I did the entire movement) we ate.

I was reimbursed in a week.

"You are just like your father." – Cheryl Ann Allen

"No, I am not. I do not smoke the same cigars, I do not wear the same bow ties and just because we are both in show business has nothing to do with it." – Ian Finkel

This page has been left blank so that the reader may gaze upon my face.

Names & Brains

My mother named me and my brother Anglo-Saxon names, Ian Lawrence and Elliot Brian.

Recently, I asked my mother, "Why the Gentile names? Why not Abe or Morris or Aaron or any other normal Jewish name?" She told me that when we were born, she was afraid that when the Nazis or Communists came to New York they would know we were Jewish. I told her, "You think the 'Finkel' at the end would be a giveaway?" She's like the scared Jew who flies Syrian Airlines to the Middle East and orders the kosher meal.

And my mother is the most intelligent person in the whole family. She can argue on any side of any topic. And win. She devours whole books in hours. Her interests are wide and deep. I always wanted to be smarter than my mother. When I was in the sixth grade, there was a mandatory IQ test given in the New York Public Schools. Why is anybody's guess, but all sixth graders had to take it. I scored 189! Naturally, the test givers thought that somehow I cheated, so they called my mother up and told her to bring me down to take the test again the next day. I did not cheat. I was IQ smart, which by the way means nothing in music. I know guys that cannot spell their own middle names that play like wizards and gods.

My mother brought me back to the school the next day. I retook the test. This time I scored 192! The test givers gave me the same stupid test! The school made me enter the special persons program that takes you from seventh grade to ninth, skipping the eighth. I failed every class they had, even with my brilliant mother, who was smarter than me, helping all the time. Still, I was pushed into high school where I was the youngest in the class. There, I failed everything as well (except for music, band, orchestra and sheet metal shop) and when I left high school all I had was a cheap drum set, a battered trumpet and a General Diploma, which meant I passed gym and shop.

The xylophone changed my life from dummy to cute-genius-virtuoso-great one. In the 1950s, my father was asked to change his name, Fyvush was too Jewish. Now, of course, any name works, if you get work, but back in the 1950s his agent suggested he change it from Fyvush Finkel to Phil Fine. Phil Fine!! How lounge lizard is that?!

"And here he is, folks! The comedy stylings of Phil Fine."

"Give him a great big hand! Phil Fine, ladies and gentlemen!"

"C'mon back! Keep it going for the comedy and song of Phil Fine!"

My father showed up at a hotel in the Catskills to work and while he was checking in at the front desk the owner came over to him and said in Yiddish, but I'll translate, "What is your name?"

My dad replied, "I'm Phil Fine."

"No, you're not."

"Yes, I am! I'm Phil Fine!"

"I hired through the agent a new comic called Phil Fine. You're Fyvush Finkel; you were here a month ago."

"But now I'm Phil Fine."

"Get out. I'm calling the agent! You're not Phil Fine."

So my father's new name lasted a week and he wisely went back to Fyvush Finkel.

Now when you walk with him on the street he is stopped constantly by adoring fans "Muhammad Ali" style. They love him. His name is cool. Well, after all, he did star in *Picket Fences*, for which he won an Emmy Award, and *Boston Public,* amongst many other shows.

After I left high school, I quickly realized I had a lot of musical learning to do. I had read somewhere that we only use ten percent of our brain, which, of course, is baloney. I use one hundred percent of it and here is how I do it.

I leave a greater portion of my brain blank. I don't think of anything except music. So I have lots of mental shelf space to use at anytime, at least ninety percent, so I keep on filling it up with music. Nothing much else.

My Brain: 90% music
            5 % for food, cigars
            2 1/2% how to be cute
            2 1/2% empty at all times in case of emergency

This page has been left blank to show the
reader the magic of computers.

The Green Spray
(Puntarenas, Costa Rica)

I was brought up to know many things. My parents instilled in me a wealth of knowledge to take me through life. For example, my father taught me about politics at the very tender of age of eleven. He took me by the hand into our living room and said, "All politicians are crooks. All!"

"Thanks, Dad!" I said. And that said it all.

My father's devotion to television bordered on religious. To him, getting on television meant making it in showbiz and we watched everything that was on, every night, as long as it was "entertainment," Ed Sullivan, *Colgate Comedy Hour*, any movie, even if we had seen it millions of times, had to be seen again and again and discussed. When my father sat down to watch the great ones on TV, to which he aspired, that was it and that's all. In those days all you could get was channels 2, 4, 5, 7, 9, 11 and 13. But, to my dad, that was enough.

My mother, on the other hand, was bright and loved education and was beside herself when they were going to televise the first man on the Moon. She sat my brother and me down to see it and exclaimed, "Think of it, a man on the Moon." And then she went on about the implications, both scientific and social, about it. My father walked in and went to the TV set. He flipped through all the channels from 2 to 13 and saw that the same thing was on every station. "Feh! Why don't they put on a regular show?!" he said and then went downstairs to smoke a cigar.

From that, I learned, and surely agree, that the space program is a waste. All that money. You go to the Moon, you bring back grey rocks...to Mars...red rocks!...Pluto...purple rocks?! Hey, how about some of that dough to cure a few diseases which have existed since then and the balance to out-of-work xylophonists?

But one thing both of my parents agreed on was *cleanliness*; not just in your act, I'd never do a blue joke, but, most importantly, cleanliness in the home, especially in the toilet. I have been told that no one says the word "toilet" quite like I do and my pronunciation should be in the Oxford English Dictionary.

I have grown up with the burning fact that the toilet is a sacred place, two locks on the door, and being clean is the only way to live. It was drummed into me to wash my hands the second I come into the apartment and I always have. I love being clean. I admit that I am afraid of deep water (hence, I wound up on cruise ships), so I do not take baths (three inches I consider deep). I take fourteen showers a day and brush and gargle at least six times. If I took a bath, I would need three people to hold me up so I do not drown.

My dad (with Mom in tow) toured and, before he made it, probably stayed in some questionable joints as all performers had to. So cleanliness was a big thing and, as all students know, history repeats itself.

So here is the dirty underbelly of cruise ships. I like a clean place to work. They are not. Oh, yes, they are always swabbing the deck, washing the tables, vacuuming, dusting, etc., but this is what I have experienced.

You get on a luxury liner bound for the Panama Canal in Fort Lauderdale, Florida. After the ship leaves the port and you are a prisoner, you get a note under your cabin door stating that the ship has NOR-WALK disease and do not shake hands, touch nothing, "be careful," whatever that means, and tough luck, sucker.

My dad would grab his bags and leave the next day. I need the money, so I stay, flip out and fill a spray bottle (I carry many sundries and such in my suitcase) with winter-green rubbing alcohol; it's about a dollar and thirteen cents a pint in any drugstore and is really seventy percent alcohol, hand sanitizers are sixty percent. For a week I spray my hands constantly. After every elevator button, pepper grinder, everything. On that cruise, three hundred passengers got ill, some leaving early, and about a hundred crew. The crew illnesses are never reported in the news. Each day, after my room steward makes up my room, I go over everything with my green spray. I never get sick unless I'm forced to listen to the score of *Cats*.

All the room stewards on this line are Indonesians. They are overworked (14 hours a day) and are kept four to a smallish cabin. Their hygiene is scant and I am sorry to indelicately say, most have terrible body odor. The room stewards do a great job, but entertainers do not get cabins with verandas and there is no way to air the room out after they "clean it." So after the Steward leaves, I light up a Partagas Robusto, fill the room with smoke, and go over everything with my green spray.

At one of the many bars on board, I sit holding my spray bottle, waiting to be asked, "What'll you have?" The bartender (on this line they are Filipino, and a great bunch of guys, though they love cockfighting and read magazines about that cruelty) sees the spray bottle and inquires as to what it is. I ask him to hold out his hands. He does and I spray them. Then I order a drink. He laughs and sprays me back! He's got an atomizer of orange water.

The ship arrives in Costa Rica and several entertainers and I go for a walk. A few blocks from the ship is the local disco-whorehouse–bar and who do we see coming out, but our room steward. "Wash your hands before you do my room!" I trill and spray him up and down. My mother would be so proud of me. And my father.

All of the Indonesians are devout Muslims and have their own mosque and dining room on the ship. Yet, I see thirty or forty at a clip frequenting every whorehouse in every port we stop at. Some are very candid about it. They've told me they love the "girls" and back home in Jakarta they'd get their hands cut off for less. When I have asked them about AIDS, they just shrug it off as in, "What do you mean?" What do I mean?!! Half the world is dying of it and *what do I mean?* The hookers, on the other hand, "love 'em." They have told me (they love to spill the beans) that the Indonesian men are small and go rather quickly. They pay for an hour and are done in ten minutes. The whole thing saddens me greatly. I, of course, do not pass judgment, but the world's oldest profession still rules the high seas.

If there is any humor in this, I can't see it. Well, one instance does come to mind. There is a bar-disco-whorehouse in Cozumel, Mexico. It is called Café Salsa. Apparently, the prices are low and the place fills up with crew by ten a.m.! Business was so good that the owner-pimp saw fit to send a bus to the ship's dock to bring his clientele to the place. The bus is parked on the dock and about thirty elderly guests, mostly from the Bible Belt, get on assuming it is the shuttle into town. Upon arrival, at the Café Salsa, they get off the bus and go in thinking it is another gift shop–rest stop. When they get in, all hell breaks loose and they run out screaming, catching cabs back to the ship to complain. Well, not all went back, seven men and two ladies remained. I would have loved to have sprayed them.

"I want the people to love me, but I suppose they never will."
—Woodrow Wilson

"There was a president that played the xylophone?"
– Ian Finkel

This page has been left blank so the reader can admire my cuteness.

People Are the Same All Over the World
(Kusadasi, Turkey - Buenos Aires, Argentina – Venice, Italy - New York, New York)

I love everyone, I hate everyone. All people of the world have the same hopes and desires, a family, a decent job, peace, a few of my CDs, good food, a '57 Buick. Even pigeons are similar everywhere. In Kusadasi, Turkey, the birds are everywhere, raining their business on one and all. There is a doughnut stand in the middle of the town's square that has the sweetest fried dough in the world. One bite and you need a root canal. Too bad there are swastikas graffitied on the walls. But the dumb dirty birds deface those evil marks as well. In New York, we have enough flying rats to spread disease for one hundred years. San Marco Square in Venice has tens of thousands of the beasts. The champion pigeons are in the Plaza de Mayo Square in front of the Casa Rosada in Buenos Aires (Evita! Evita!) This is the Square where, since 1977, on every Thursday, you can see the Madres (mothers) of the Plaza de Mayo march in a large circle. They hold up photos of their missing loved ones, mostly children, who were taken in the night. This is their act of demanding answers and justice. Justice has yet to come. There are silhouettes on the ground of lost Argentineans. The tourists love to lay down in them and have their picture taken. The entire scene rips your heart out. As for the pigeons, you throw corn at them, which is sold there for next to nothing, and a layer of the dirty birds come down and they feed like a pack of starving actors. Then you throw some more and another million of them go on top of the first layer forming an undulating carpet of pigeons with feathers, excretions, dust and God knows what else churning everywhere. A great place to diet as you will lose your desire to eat for a month.

But humans make the birds seem clean. In Kusadasi, I change a twenty-dollar bill for Turkish Lira, I get back millions. Can't they cut off a few zeros? I do not know how much I have. There is a poor street beggar and I give him what I think is a large alm and he starts to scream at me. I yell back at him that I just gave him one hundred and fifty thousand Liras and he spits on me in Turkish disgust.

"Are you crazy, you stupid idiot?!" I yell.

A passerby stops and taps me on the shoulder. Gently he says to me, "You just gave him ten cents, my friend. I apologize for his behavior and our money." I give the beggar all the money I have and I give the passerby a cigar.

I returned to the ship to think.

Argentina is "meat world." Every meal has meat, meat soup, meat appetizer, meat meat, meat dessert and meat coffee. On San Francisco Street, there are wonderful stores and restaurants. There is a music store where I bought some wonderful Tango arrangements. It also had not one but two copies of a book I wrote thirty years ago. Amazing. It had the old price on it so I could see that it had been there for years. There is no vehicular traffic on the street as it really is a mall and because of this there are Tango dancers, people hawking all kinds of things and sadly, children who have been taught to beg while playing the small accordion. Very tragic.

There was a little girl, no more than four years old, sitting on the ground playing her instrument. I stopped and looked at her. Though I cannot speak Spanish, I knelt down and softly told her, "You play wonderfully. Here is your pay," and I gave her a dollar. She took the bill and held it up to the light and then she spit in my face. I wiped it off with my sleeve and stood up. What I thought might be her older brother came over and said, "I am sorry, senor, but she hate American."

I gave him three dollars and a small but fine cigar; after all, he looks to be only about ten years old. He was delighted and said, "Thank you (muchas gracias), senor!"

I returned to the ship to think.

I am home in New York and I am driving up Third Avenue. At 53rd Street, I stopped for a red light. It turned green, but there was a sweet elderly lady that was still crossing the intersection slowly. She raised her hand as if to make the traffic wait and we come into eye contact. I waved to her in a gesture of, "Take your time, go slowly." She made an angry face and spit on my windshield. I rolled down the window and yelled, "Are you Turkish? Do you play accordion?!!!"

I drove home, parked and went to bed, to think.

This page has been left blank to allow the reader time to reflect on the material thus far.

The End of the Line

You really don't see too many old-time showbiz types around anymore. If you watch an award show, you will see that they are not there. An actor wins, he goes up to accept and he barely can speak in front of a live audience. Void of any wit or charm, most of them collect their winnings and shuffle off. When my dad won his Emmy for *Picket Fences*, he was great. After that night, people would come up to me and say, "They don't make 'em like that anymore!"

"A real old trooper."

"The last of the Shmohawks." (Some were trying to be funny.)

I started to think (which is a bad move) . . . wait a minute! I have to carry on that tradition:

1. Being cordial to the fans. (I make believe I have more than just the people from the cruises.)

2. Knowing what to say to the audience when winning an award. ("And in the category of xylophone virtuoso, the winner, and only contestant is . . .")

3. Having good clean fun when on the road with my peers.

4. Love the whole damn thing of it. (Though I don't want to be loved back.)

I look at my father as a member of Royalty. In the way he carries himself. The way he talks to his fans. Not condescendingly, but as if they are his dearest friends, and they are. When he is out with anyone, no one touches their money. A star takes his "boys" with him.

But wait a minute! Again!! That's what I do. The only difference is, in my father's day, there was a show business, now there's not. It's all accountants, lawyers, know-it-alls and know-it-nothings. But I do try to carry myself like a star. Keep the element of fun for all.

It is hard with some of the new acts, though. I find I have less and less to talk about with them. I actually met an act, a magician who shall be nameless, that did not know who Laurel and Hardy were! Can you imagine that? How would you like it if I went up to a baseball fan and confessed that I had never heard of Babe Ruth?!!! The stupid S.O.B.! The only way to really know if something is good is to know where it came from. No wonder his act stunk. I watched a rerun of the old *Ed Sullivan Show* and saw a magician do this guy's whole forty-five-minute act in six minutes!!

I was orchestrating a production show years ago and the choreographer wanted me to write a number for two male dancers that slide out onto the stage and jump over the band, etc. I asked him, "Oh, you mean like the Nicholas Brothers?"

And he replied, "Who are they?"

Wherever he is now I am sure that he is pumping gas as well as he choreographed.

Even though it is a small portion of show business as it is now, I keep up the legacy of the old-time greats. That doesn't mean I play dated stuff, I keep on adding new things all the time.

There may not be too many places to work, but I keep up the traditions. A prince in exile. Okay, a Baron in exile. Oh, all right already, a knave in exile!

"Know thine opportunity." – Pittacus

"I beeped where I should have bopped." – Ian Finkel

This page has been left blank to facilitate page turns(as in music).

Ship of Fools At Sea

All entertainers will tell you that whenever the phone rings it makes their hearts jump. Not me! I monitor all my calls and listen to the playbacks, this way I can study them and plan out what I am going to say. Years ago before answering machines, I would rush to the phone thinking each call was the one that would offer me my dream job, a combination of *The Jackie Gleason Show* and *The Bell Telephone Hour*. If you are too young to know what those shows were, let's just say, it would be a show where I do great sketch comedy and conduct and solo with an eighty-piece orchestra, made up of New York's finest freelance symphony musicians.

Of course, that call never came. Instead, the phone would ring and I'd lunge at it and answer, "Hello! This is Ian Finkel, The World's Greatest Xylohonist. I am available for weddings, Bar or Bas Mitzvahs and meat market openings. Can I help you?"

"Mister Finkel?" (It's the voice of another life-shortener.) "Ah yes, this is Irving Feininsteinblatto at LSMABC securities. How are you today?"

"I'm all right." (I feel myself getting frail.)

"What? Well, Mr. Finkel. . .May I call you Ian?" He pronounces it Eey-an.

"I'm all right, and it's Eye-an."

"Well, Eeyan, here it is. We here at LSMABC Securities, have come upon a great deal that I think will change the way you make money."

"I don't make money. I earn it."

"Ha, ha, yes. . .if you just hear me out. You see, for a small investment of, let's say, ten thousand dollars, after a short period of, let's say, six to eight weeks, I can assure you that your share in this development of future investment of property and air sickness bag manufacturing will bear the fruits of at least fifty to one hundred times the initial investment and after our very modest commission you will see that the future will turn over to you the tidy sum, in regular checks, of anywhere from six million to eight million dollars and, if you give me a few more moments of your time, I can go into the details of this exciting offer!!"

"I like fruit, room temperature."

"Well, of course, so do I! Now, Eeyan, shall I put you down for ten thousand?"

"No. Make it double! I'll give you twenty!" I didn't have my rent that month.

"Twenty!!! Good, great, I mean, of course, a man with your insight and. . ."

"But, naturally," I insert, "you will invest an equal amount into my next recording."

"What?"

"Look, man, I don't know you and you call me up and want ten thousand from me. That's fine, but, naturally, I want to give you the same opportunity as a thank you. In fact, my next album is entitled *Antarctican Love Songs*. It's basically a tribute to Frank Sinatra on solo xylophone. Maybe I'll add some banjo and accordion interludes and though it may start off a bit cold, I am sure the Sinatra name will make it go gold and possibly heat it up to platinum. Maybe I should put you down for twenty?"

He hangs up. So do I.

So I now monitor my calls. The phone rings, it is my agent. This one I pick up.

"Hello, Melinda. . .I'll take it!"

"Hello, Ian (Eye-an). I just got a call from the Cunard Line. You were such a solid hit on two of their ships that they want you on their third one. It's called the Vistafiord. It leaves in a week for the Mediterranean and they have a great eight-piece band. The money is the same and the job is for three weeks."

"Okay, where do I fly to?"

"You pick up the ship in Venice."

I flew to Italy and got to the ship. It looked old and rusty. I got on and signed in at the desk. No one greeted me or anything. I went to my cabin. It's the last one on the lowest inhabitable deck. The floor had a twenty-degree angle; well, after all, it is at the end of the ship. I put a few ashtrays under my xylophone to level it and practiced with one shoe on and one shoe off. Two days went by and no one called. I could have gone to the Cruise Director's office to introduce myself, but I am the "star" of the ship and they should come and say hello to me. I stayed in my slanty cabin, ate some room service and, on the third day I got a note under my door saying, "REHEARSAL THREE P.M. SHOW AT EIGHT."

I went to the rehearsal. The ballroom–theatre was old shabby and the lighting and sound man was one. I gave him my three pages of lighting cues. (I, of course, said hello first and introduced myself.) He was a child of eighteen.

He looked at the pages of cues and said, "We have very little equipment here, the best I can do with the lights is on or off. I'll set up your mikes."

I went up on stage and greeted the band. They are from Poland and speak almost no English. Seven sidemen have the name of Marick. The leader, who was the pianist, spoke a little English and his name was Roman as in Polanski. Fine. We handed out my music and began. A half an hour later, we were still on the first eight bars of the opening number. Dear Lord, they stunk! I did the best I could and got through the rehearsal.

At seven-forty-five, I was dressed and waiting off stage in a closet-size kind of dressing room. My xylophone was, of course, waiting for me onstage. The door to the closet flew open and in walked a very large, blonde, blue-eyed Bruenhilda type. No hello. Nothing. She made straight for me and said in thick heavy German accent, "How vould you like for me to introduce you?"

I was thinking, "Okay, she is obviously the Cruise Director," but a small hello would have been nice. I looked up at her, she is over six-foot-five, I am five-ten, and I said, "Well, just say that he is the star instrumentalist of the Cunard Line, the World's Greatest Xylophonist and here he is, Ian Finkel."

"I am not going to say that!"

Now, normally, any emcee will say whatever the act wants, but this was something new to me. So I just said, "Why not?"

"Because I do not know that you are the world's greatest zyll-loff-phone-ist."

I wanted to say, "But, I am. . .and drop dead. . .and I'm not going on," etc., but, instead, said, "Well, then say what you want."

She turned briskly and left. Eight PM. Showtime. The band played Bruenhilda on with "The Girl from Ipanema." It sounded more like a march than a Bossa-Nova. She began speaking to the audience for twenty minutes in German.

"Guttenaven mein liebe fraint," etc.

It hit me. . .hard. . .they don't speak English. What would I say to them between numbers? How could I be cute? After the twenty minutes, she said in English, "He is from New York and he plays the zyll-loff-phone. He is from the New York City, Eeyan *Fin* kel."

I made my entrance. I kicked off Roman and the seven Maricks. They sounded horrid. I finished my opener. There was very little applause at the end. I heard the audience murmuring. Then it hit me again. . .harder. They are old, very old; I could see that the audience was mostly in their seventies and eighties. They are predominantly German. . .and, believe me, I was not paranoid, but I was sure they hated Jews.

I do not hate any race. I only hate specific individuals. But I could feel the bad taste coming off of them. Well, if they were still fighting World War II that was their problem.

I went quickly into my second sure-fire number, "The Flight of the Bumble Bee Rhumba." I do everything in it. I come just short of hitting the floor at the last chord and screaming "Mammy" a la Jolson. (Whoops, another Jew.) Thirteen people stood up and left. How did I know it was thirteen? I counted them. In my mind, I went one Mississippi, two Mississippi, three, etc., until thirteen.

I remembered my father teaching me that when you once in a rare while get an audience that disliked you, "Go through your act to the finish. There is always someone there that will like you. Give it your all. That is the professional way."

So I kept going.

Two numbers later, I got to the end of my Gershwin (again a Jew) Medley. Twenty-five got up and left. How did I know it was twenty-five? I counted them. One Mississippi, two Mississippi, through to twenty-five. But, I forged ahead.

At the end I walked off to a half house and tepid applause. I returned to the closet dressing room. I sat down. For the first time in my life, I was covered in flop sweat.

Bruenhilda flung the door open and marched in like she was taking the Sudetenland all over again. She grinned and said, "Verrry Goodt!"

I lost it. "What?!! Are you kidding?! Did you see the same show I just did?! And what the hell kind of intro was that?! Look here, lady, I *am* the World's Greatest Xylophonist and. . . ."

Before I said anything more, she threw her head back and said,

"That's the vay ve Germans are." And then the quick turn and she left.

I went to the phone and called my agent in New York. I told her that this ship was a lousy Bundt meeting. I bombed and I'm leaving in the morning."

"But, Ian, it's three days to the next port and we signed for three weeks. Do the best you can."

"But the band is Lech Walessa's house band. It's a nightmare. They are from Poland. They don't speak English, they can't play my stuff and when I get back to New York you'll need new office furniture because I'm gonna trash your place because you sent me here!!"

She laughed and hung up. The phone call, ship to shore, was $136.13.

The gig dragged on. No one spoke to me. The food was horrible. If I ever see another wiener snitchel-spatzel meal again, I'll become a vegan.

Six days later, I got another note under the door of my slanted cabin. "REHEARSAL AT THREE, SHOW AT EIGHT."

Okay! I prepared an evening of classical music for the audience to enjoy. I rehearsed and the band was much better at the accompaniment of my medley of Strauss Waltzes than they were at Mambo-Jambo six days earlier.

My Wagnerian beauty intros me and I went out. There were a mere forty people in the audience. Only some British people who made the mistake of taking this ship instead of the QE2. A small but decent group, they got everything and it went well.

Where were the bulk of the people? I found out later that opposite me in the movie house on board they showed the German version of *Schindler's List*. It was renamed *Happy Days*.

The next two weeks went by slowly, but I made it. I disembarked in Denmark. Don't ask me how we got there. I was so happy to leave, that while I waited for the van to take me to the airport, I was kissing the ground like the Pope. The Valkyrie Lady passed me on the dock and as she waved she said, "Ta, ta, you'll be back!"

And I answered her with every Deutschland über alles line I could think of, ending the whole tirade with a Yiddish translation of "I'll be glad when you're dead, you rascal you."

Home again. The phone rang and it was my agent. "Hi, Ian, I just got a call from Cunard. They want you back for a month on the Vistafiord."

There is a saying about cruise ship acts. If you are a hit, you'll be back. If you lay an egg, you'll be back sooner. I, of course, declined the engagement.

A month went by and I got a call from an old pal. He is a very fine ventriloquist. I have appeared with him many times and, come to think of it, on the two good Cunard ships as well.

"Hey, Ian!"

"Hey, Jerry"

"Listen to this. I got a call from my agent and he said there was an opening on the Vistafiord. Some act declined the offer so since I was a liberty I took the job."

I wanted to vomit, but let him go on.

"And here is what happened: I got some cabin that the floor was a hill. The band was terrible and the Cruise Director, some huge tank of a thing, introduced me for twenty minutes in German. Then says, 'Here he is, I forget his name.' I go out with my old man puppet and do the first joke. I hear nothing! Just silence."

I wanted to tell him that he should have called me first and I would have told him not to do the job, they don't speak English, they're rude, should-ah, would-ah, could-ah, but I let him go on.

"So I go into my second gag with the puppet. Now I hear crickets chirping."

I start to feel numb, but I let him go on.

"Now I get freaked and realize they don't really speak English and before I go into the third joke an old guy in the audience gets up and shouts at me, 'Vas is Das, Sprecken zee deucht!' So I ask my puppet,

'Do you speak German?' and he answers, 'No, Jerry I don't.' So I say to the audience, 'Goodnight, everybody!' and walk off."

I can't feel my lips, but I manage to say, "Then what?"

"Well, the Cruise Director runs on stage, tells the band to play some dance music and, well, I flew home the next morning."

"Good Gosh."

"And, of course, my agent said that Cunard will never use me again on any of their ships. I think I lost the whole Cunard account."

I lit up a fresh cigar and said, "Jerry, don't worry, they'll want you back!"

All This for $500 A Night
(Papeete, Tahiti)

This place is French. Perhaps that accounts for the amazing rip-offs and hatred for Americans that exists there. Four of us entertainers got off in Papeete to fly home to the United States. We left the ship at ten in the morning and would make our way to the hotel to spend the night. The next day would be a thousand-hour plane ride to the States. My "peers" were a husband and wife magic act and a Country Western singer. The singer's name was Darleen. I swear that she had never been anywhere other than Nashville, was born and will probably end there as well. She seemed so dumb that I could imagine her peeling an M&M candy while driving a bright red pickup truck. How did she get the booking? The audiences on the ship were tough. I, however, killed. We had had several long runs of sea days, and six in a row without a port is normal for that part of the world, just look at a map.

Darleen hated everything and her complaining was lethal. The magicians, whose name was something like the Great Magnetos or Magnettis, wanted her dead from the first day we all met. Darleen put down the ship, food, the band, you name it, and The Great Magnetos were the old school types who were gracious and polite, about everything. As for myself, I hate everyone and everything, but I am charming around the other performers as all stars should be.

We left the ship and miraculously our luggage was taken on ahead. We were told we had time to shop around for an hour and there were plenty of stands at the dock selling everything. Papeete is an epicenter of transgender. Why this place, I don't know, but everyone selling something was at least a six-foot-three, two-hundred-pound woman with five o'clock shadow (at ten a.m.) and an Adam's apple. So what? Who cares? Darleen went berserk.

"Hey, y'all, look at 'em!" she loudly cried as she slapped my back.

"Look at what?" Mr. Magneto said.

"They's all roosters made into hens! For Lord's sake!" Darleen said and slapped harder.

"Oh, c'mon," I whispered. "Haven't you ever had capon?"

"What?"

The Magnetos discretely chuckled and we moved around the stalls. We stopped at a fishmonger and Darleen could not control herself. "That there fella or whatever he is, well, I just wouldn't eat what he's a-cutting up!"

The lady in question was close to seven feet tall, with jet-black hair, a beautiful Asian.

"Oh, please, keep your comments to yourself," Mr. Magneto said.

"Indeed," echoed Mrs. Magneto.

I walked around the table to get next to the fish seller. I went up on my toes and whispered, "Please ignore her. She has never been anywhere. You are very beautiful and if we were to stay here I'd buy one of your fine fish and cook it and enjoy it."

The seven-foot giantess said in a husky, mannish tone, "You are pleased to go away. Customers only now and thank you."

The cab dropped us off in paradise, a hotel on the side of a mountain. The rooms? $500 a night! The Magnetos "oohed" and "ahhed" and we went to the desk to check in. The desk attendants, concierge and various other workers, were all tall, thin, beautiful women with slight five o'clock shadows and Adam's apples. (Since then, I've heard that the "apple" can be shaved a bit down to make the neck feminine.) My neck is quite lovely.

Our rooms were fine and I called Marty back in New York to tell him what a big hit I was. (I'd later find out that the eight minutes I talked would cost $152.13.) We all met for lunch in the hotel's restaurant. Of course, all the waiters were transsexuals and Darleen went nuts. I stepped on her foot under the table and said, "Look here, you Okey from Muskogee, they'll mishandle our eats. You don't want to eat, that's your business, but we want to, so, please, sugar, be quiet. Okay?" And I pressed my foot upon hers a bit harder. That did the trick and the food was good, French, but good.

The hotel had an open lobby and floors, no doors, few walls. The French can be frugal. The mountain air breezed around and you could sit on fine leather furniture, but at the same time get the feel of being in the open air. The cost of a room was five hundred a night U.S. Ooh la la.

After lunch, I found out that there was a cigar store in town and I herded my peers into a cab. "We'll look around."

The cab took us into town and it had thinned out due to the ship leaving. We sat at an outdoor café and had espressos, which were fine. The cigar store was there and in we went. The shopkeeper was a short French lady, a Piaf in her dotage, about fifty-five years old and Darleen lit up.

"Well, now, ain't you the cutest lady in the Pacific," she said. The owner eyed her up and down and raised her chin up. Not in the noble fashion, but rather in the French way. The French rise up their chins when they smell a bad Camembert or are approached by an American.

I looked over the cigars in the case. Okay stuff and I saw a few Dominicans I had had in New York a week before that were good. In New York they were six bucks apiece.

"How much are these, Madame?" I asked.

"Forty-eight, Monsieur," she replied.

"For a box?" I asked.

"No, no, Monsieur, forty-eight each!"

"Francs?" My mouth went dry.

"United States Dollar," she answered.

Darleen jumped up in place, she turned purple and shouted, "Forty-eight dollars a smoke? Are you pullin' our laygs? Honey, are those made by Charlie De Gawl hisself?"

The Magnetos beat a retreat out into the street. The petite lady rose up and declared, "Madame, these are from the isle of the Dominican Republic. We are many miles from that part of zee world."

"Honey, in the next war you can fend for yourselves!" said Darleen as she walked out and waited on the street with the Magnetos. I stood there and blushed. I was about to come up with a clever exit line, but the French lady stood her ground and said to me, "Perhaps Monsieur would like to purchase a small package of chewing gum."

Back to the hotel for me.

The Island became dark and the lights went on all over the hotel. Since the lobby and succeeding floors were open to the elements, the elements came to the hotel, moths, millions of 'em, all shapes and South Pacific sizes, flying this way and that, with no possibility of a truce. The four of us were sitting in the lobby having a drink as darkness fell and the lights of the hotel came on. The first winged insect went for a swim in Darleen's drink and she poured the drink out into a potted palm tree.

"This here place is too buggy for me. I'm goin' to my room."

"Good idea," commented Mr. Magneto, but he and his wife sat still. I looked out toward the mountains. You could see the clouds of moths formulating and zeroing in for the attack.

"Lord A' mighty here they come!" roared Darleen and she was correct. Within minutes, the damn things were flying everywhere and it was impossible to relax and finish our drinks. The staff moved around the lobby soundlessly and continued their work without any notice of the bugs.

"Perhaps it is time to go to our rooms," Mrs. Magneto said, "as it is a bit too buggy for us as well."

"Yes, indeed, my dear, we should go," added Mr. Magneto and they rose up. Then it happened. As the Magnetos rose up and pushed their chairs back, from under their seats emerged an army of white lizards. The things freaked me out and I stood up. The lizards, gecko like, ran everywhere, up and down the walls and couches, up the lamps, on the front desk and under tables and chairs. One jumped onto Darleen's lap. She screamed a scream that woke up her pet hogs back in Tennessee.

"Yeehaaaaah!"

It was obvious to me that the geckos checked in to eat the moths. And, may I say, a smorgasbord was laid out for them. They feasted and we ran to our rooms.

But then a problem came up. As the four of us ran to our rooms that were on the same floor, the hallway was a wind tunnel of moths and the geckos were in hot pursuit. How does one open his door and get in his room without letting in the moths and lizards?

"Oh Lord, I never did anything to deserve this!" Darleen cried.

"Perhaps it was your show," Mrs. Magneto snapped and she and her husband swiftly were gone. Darlene was freaked. Quickly, I lit up my last cigar. I fired the thing up and the clouds of blue smoke surrounded me. I stood by my door, puffing until a good cloud cover was formed and I opened my door and went in. Only two moths made it in and I swatted them to their reward. I ran to my suitcase and got out a roll of gaffers tape I always carry for the repair of luggage. I taped up the door's circumference and was safe. No room service tonight for me.

I got a water glass from the bathroom and waited about a minute. I heard the next room door slam. Then I put the glass to the wall, my ear to the glass, and enjoyed the show. Darleen's moans and screams were a delight. What marvelous dialogue. "Damn! Gotcha! There's another one! Oh you devil, get offa my bed! Damn, ooh, ahh."

Then came the best, "Eeeek! Get offa me you slimy thang!" That night, I slept with a grin on my face.

"He who is shipwrecked the second time cannot lay the blame on Neptune." – English Proverb

"Cruise ship captains do it all the time." – Ian Finkel

The Flying Dutchman
(Off the Coast of Greenland)

If there is a place as silly as Greenland anywhere else in the world, I'd like to know about it so I can go there by ship and vomit hundreds of times with my fellow passengers and band.

Once a year I get on a ship that leaves from New York (there aren't many that still do) and it's easy. I live ten minutes from the 48th Street dock and the dockworkers there are good guys who help me with my bags and cases. Let me point out that these are *American* dockworkers. They know I'm not De Niro. Some think I'm Pavarotti, so on occasion I sing them a bop version of "Nessen Dorma." When I sing, I sound like Jerry Lewis doing Carol Channing. I can dance, too, but after many years on the stage I realize that there is only one move that works for me, it's my "Pump the Rhino – Shuffle the Shovel." Someday, I'll pass it on, maybe to the City Ballet.

The ship goes up the side of the U.S. stopping at Rhode Island (good clams), Boston (good fish), St. John's, Canada (great coffee houses), and then three ports in Greenland that are unpronounceable and are beyond ridiculous. There is not much to see, unless you take a tour of the glaciers (which all look the same to me) and the locals sell small hand carvings that are amateurish for sixty dollars. The guests complain endlessly about Greenland. So why do they go? Maybe they lie in wait for the European ports that are further down the line. The ship is a massive, twelve-story Dutch wonder and seems to move smoothly from port to port. There are two sea days after the third Greenland port and then we get to Reykjavik, Iceland, where I'm supposed to get off and fly back to New York, spend a day home and then fly to Los Angeles to do the Jerry Lewis Telethon. By the way, Greenland is fifteen hundred miles of ice and Iceland is kinda green.

A storm comes up, a big one, and the ship begins to go up and down more violently with each thrust. The first day and night the passengers vomit freely any place they want, on the couches, in the theater, movie house, restaurants, everywhere. I thank the heavens I have already done my show.

(There was one night in Seoul, Korea, that some of the orchestra members threw up. I attributed that response to the mystery meat we were served at dinner between the rehearsal and the show. The audience was not in a good mood either. The show opened with a very poor singer who was booed off of the stage. So bad was this vocalist that three minutes into my act the audience began to boo him again.)

The first night of the storm, the show was cancelled as a unicyclist was scheduled and I guess that made a lot of sense. The next night was a comedian and I went to the balcony to see his act. The ship heaved and thrust and there were only eight or so people in the nine-hundred-seat theater. As the ship lurched and raised up, the comedian sat down on the stage, fearful that he might fall if he remained standing up. He told a Mexican joke (we are off the coast of Greenland!) and then there was a great impact and I was thrown out of my seat. Within ten seconds, water entered the balcony from God knows where and started to cascade down the steps to the orchestra seats below. The water seeped into the millions of wires and I heard a zzz-zzz sound. The lights flickered wildly. The water was ankle high and I raised my feet up as not to get electrocuted. The comic who had been tossed into the front row seats began to tell a lifeboat joke. The Cruise Director (who is in charge of the shows) ran up the steps to the balcony, fighting the Niagara effect, to where I was sitting.

"Stop the show," I said, "or we'll all be electrocuted!"

"Should I?" he answered.

"What?" you stupid wimp! "Stop the show. Get everyone out of here...now!" I command.

"Well, the hotel manager wants a full show every night and..." Then there was another loud crash of impact, followed by a crackling sound.

In my best imitation of Butterfly McQueen, I called out, "Oh, Lawdy, we go-na-die!"

Everyone ran out of the theater and all the lights went out. I headed for the center of the ship on that floor, where there was a bar and television set that showed the front of the ship. The replay was already on. Apparently, the camera at the front of the wheelhouse caught it all. A humongous fifty-foot wave of ocean blue had hit the ship head-on. You could see it coming, a gigantic wall of water, fifty feet high and one hundred feet wide. It ripped off parts of the ship, which are now at the bottom of the sea. I know these dimensions to be correct as I interviewed various officers the next day. I found out later that we could have avoided the whole thing, but the captain decided to go that way to a particular scenic area for viewing. I guess he was too busy to check the radar or the weather reports.

We were a day late getting into Iceland. I just made it to Los Angeles for the Telethon. I returned three weeks later to that Flying Dutchman and most of the theater was still in disrepair and the shows suffered greatly. Apparently, the ship's "electricians" had come to the rescue and cut all wires they could get to. Nothing worked properly, the stage lights, the moveable bandstand, the sound monitors, not much of anything. The floor of the stage seemed a bit sticky, but I still managed to "Pump the Rhino – Shuffle the Shovel."

It was tough to do a show there, even the grand piano was still damp and most entertainers had it rough. As usual, I was a hit. Saddest of all to me was that the guests hardly knew the difference. After all, most people these days that frequent those cruise ships have never paid to get in to see a real show. Some of the shows, except for mine, should pay the audience for sitting through it. Those that leave early should get a bonus.

It's Raining Volkswagens
(Off The Coast of Ecuador)

Bugs. They rule the world. I know this for a fact because I have seen it. Each year they increase in size to gigantic proportions and apparently nothing fazes them. Radiation? "Haa!" says the New York cockroach.

    A few years ago I was in Miami Beach in a parking lot that belonged to the Dezerland Hotel. The Dezerland Hotel featured vintage '50s cars in its lobby and it had a few rusted-out '59 Cadillacs in the back of the parking lot. I was crying because there before me was a 1959 Cadillac convertible rusting to death. You could see it had been originally pink with aquamarine seats. What a shame. I became angry at the hotel for letting this beautiful brontosaurus go to rust and I kicked a rusty beer can beside me under the car in anger.

    I heard the sound first, a cross between an Oster blender and a helicopter. From out of the space between a rusted fender and flat tire came the biggest, ugliest, flying devil I had ever seen, four wings, a glowing black body and a stinger that seemed to be four inches long. I took off and the B52 went after me. I started to scream and flail my arms, but it kept-on-a'comin'! I ran as fast as my 285 pounds (at the time; now, I'm a svelte 256) would go, but I knew it would catch me and sting me and I would die a horrible bloated death. My instinct took over and I grabbed my light-blue Shantung hat off of my head and threw it into the air. The insect-leer-jet went up after it and hit it dead-on. I ran into the lobby and fell upon a 1954 Studebaker. I tipped two bellhops to go out and find my hat. They couldn't. Perhaps the bug ate it.

On an overnight stay in Madeira, an island owned by Portugal, I had another encounter with death. It was two a.m. and I got up to go downstairs and out for some air. It was late so I quietly opened my hotel room door and there waiting to get in was a baseball glove-size water bug. Try to imagine a New York cockroach blown up to horror picture dimensions. I kicked the beast and it slid back about ten feet. Better to be on the offense, I went straight for it and kicked it again, this time down the stairs, which were quite long. It hit the lobby floor and made its way to a small fountain and went in and refreshed itself. The insect looked up to the top of the stairs and, seeing its master, The World's Greatest Xylophonist-Entertainer, changed its mind and took off. I went down the stairs in pursuit, but it was gone. I went to the desk and told the night manager about it. In the "Portuguese" style he just shrugged his shoulders and said, "Ah yes, Mr. Finkel, two in the morning is Pablo's exercise hour."

Off the coast of Ecuador was horrific. It was about ten o'clock at night and I was on the open upper deck of a fabulous mammoth cruise ship. We were to dock the next morning, so most of the guests had gone to bed early so as to rest up for their next long port day buying five-dollar Panama hats.

I was writing an orchestration for an opera singer who insisted that I combine "Misty" with "The Stars and Stripes Forever." That's tenors for you. At first I didn't notice the rather loud plopping, slapping sound. But after I had written a high C sharp for the lead trumpet, I looked up. Hundreds of green-black Volkswagen-sized moths were landing everywhere. Their wingspread was as wide as my six-inch ruler and the body was just as long. Plop, slap, lop, plop, slap and I gathered up my manuscript papers and quills and ran into the deck's restaurant, which was mostly empty. A few hardy teenagers were on the other side of the deck and a few of them, laughing, kicked the nightmarish things. The bugs didn't budge. I went to my room posthaste. The next day, the bugs were gone.

That night, the ship held an outdoor barbeque on that open deck. I usually do not go to the ship barbeques because that is exactly what they are not. Barbeques have meat that is slowly smoked, hours and hours, and is drowning in beautiful Texas-type sauce. These one-hour events are more like "cook outs." The grills were giving off smoke signals and hundreds of starving passengers lined up with their trays to get their fill of burnt chicken breast with raw centers and limp salad.

Pearl Harbor was then reenacted. The green-black Volkswagens fell upon us in sneak attack. The passengers' screams were deafening. The guests tried to cover their plates of food (they only had five meals so far that day) instead of their heads. I, of course, ran for cover into the restaurant and quickly ordered a pizza with extra garlic, which usually keeps vampires at bay.

> "Why should the devil have all the best tunes?"
> – Proverb 1800s

> "He doesn't, I do." – Ian Finkel

This page has been left blank to give space for notes on which cruise ship not to take.

A Brunei-Guy
(Bangkok & Pataya, Thailand, and Brunei)

I have played the xylophone for thirty-six years. In that time I have averaged three to five hours a day practice and have missed, all told, at the most, two weeks. That means that in thirty-six years I stood before the keyboard with the dedication and zeal that it takes to be a virtuoso. The worst thing you can do to an instrumental-mental case is to make him miss a day's practice. It would be the same as going to Bellevue and taking away the "busy work" (untangling small twisted chains, yarn into balls, dusting, dusting and re-dusting the library etc.), which would lead to an onslaught of screaming and crying by the inmates.

The only way a real virtuoso would miss a day's practice by choice would be by his goldfish dying or the offer of sex by anyone. But the privilege of practice can be taken away by outside forces as well and the virtuoso could be helpless to stop it.

If a musician plays a large instrument and it has to go as luggage on a plane, he is at the mercy of morons. Anything can happen and does. The airlines have lost my xylophone several times and those times have added up to the two weeks I've mentioned. Most "civilians" would not think this a big deal, but I assure you that when you miss even a day's practice, it can wreak havoc to your hands and permanent damage to your mind.

A few years ago, I flew to Cartegena, Colombia, my "favorite" place in South America, and my instrument did not appear on the carousel. It was Christmas Eve and no one was there to pick me up. No Hectors, no Uzi boys. I was all alone in the airport. Not even the office where you could report lost luggage was open. The whole airport became deserted in minutes. I found a cab and went to a hotel that I had stayed at before. Here's a tip, if you get stranded in the Caribbean, Central or the top of South America: Always go to the Caribe Grand. Every hotel is named that. The one in Cartagena has great food, monkeys, birds, and a gigantic swimming pool.

I called New York, I called the airlines that lost my xylophone and I called my best pal Marty, who basically said, "Pray hard." I waited four days for the instrument to catch up. The ship, of course, was long gone and once I got all my luggage, four days later, I had to fly back to Miami and connect to Costa Rica to catch the ship.

By the time I did my show on the ship, the four days of abstinence had done their damage and my hands were shot. My mind was putty from crying. After all, it was Chanukah and Christmas without my xylophone. By the way, the audience did not notice a thing and still gave me my usual standing ovation, which made me hate them all the more for not knowing the difference.

I got back to New York and some of my musician friends accused me of not practicing as they did notice some flaws in my playing. I have punished them many times for their lack of sympathy, leaving them in the dust via my dazzling technique.

Asia is not for me. Cigars? Forget it. Some of the food is good and hot, but it is so far away that when tragedy strikes you are done for.

I flew to Bangkok, Thailand, and the airline lost the case containing the keyboard to the xylophone. It was one a.m. and the port agency had sent a young lady about eighteen years old to whisk me to the ship, plus a driver. The young lady spoke next to nothing in English and wore no make-up. The more I cried to her, the more she became distant and confused. I called New York and my agent told me, "Don't worry. Go to the ship. It is in port overnight, two days, and the airlines will deliver it to you. If you do not go to the ship, you will not get paid! We cannot help you from here."

So I made out a report at the airport and loaded my luggage, *sans* keyboard, into the van and climbed into a backseat to cry. The young lady and driver got in the front. Through my tears, I said, "How far is the ship?"

"Ship in Pataya, three hours, please."

"Three hours?"

"Yes."

"Where is Pataya?"

"Sorry?"

"Pataya, where? How far is it?"

"Blah, ya da ya da kilometers, please."

I calculated kilometers into miles. Over one hundred. The tears rolled on. After about twenty minutes, the young lady - I never got her name, what's the difference, she couldn't help me anyway - turned around and saw me crying. She smiled largely and said, "We now pass the residence of the old King of Thailand. His name is Bhumibol Adulyadej. Can you say Bhumibol Adulyadej?"

I could not believe it. She's into the tour mode for the cruise ship passengers. "No, I can't say it! Leave me alone!"

Ignoring me, she continued, "Our good King played the saxophone tenor. He was very good. Can you say saxophone tenor?"

I dried my tears and screamed at her, "No, I will not say saxophone tenor, and besides, you torturess, your King played the alto saxophone! Can you say alto saxophone?!!" She turned around and faced front. "And, and, and, I heard the old son of a bitch wasn't that good an alto saxophonist and was a poor sight reader and though all the famous jazz cats came over here to take his money, eat his food, and kiss his behind, they personally told me that he stunk on his alto. Can you say STUNK?!"

She remained silent for the next two hours. We got to the ship at four a.m. At eight I woke the Cruise Director and told her of my lost keyboard and that I could not do the show until it arrived. She couldn't have cared less. Since we were in port for the day, staying until eleven at night, I looked around. All ships stay at least two days in Pataya. That is because it is the world's biggest whorehouse on the planet. You walk down the street and see the officers, crew, other entertainers; you name it, going into the bar-whorehouses. You see aged Japanese businessmen walking the streets with two young thirteen-year-old girls or boys, or both. I got the info on the place. Bring a thousand or two and you can rent a house with cook and have twenty-four-hour-a-day hookers to stay with you and do whatever. The World's Greatest Xylophonist without his instrument in the world's biggest whorehouse. I felt nauseous and went back to the ship. I thought about what poverty does to a people. Horrifying.

Naturally, the ship left that night and, of course, the keyboard in its case never came, two days at sea, no port. I called from the ship to my agent, the airlines and Marty. I cried to one and all. Marty's basic reaction was "Let them drop dead. Come home, 'cause, boy, you in a heap o'trouble!"

And when a Jewish New York drummer says that line, in a faux southern good ole boy accent . . . well, you are in a heap!

The two days at sea felt like a year in prison. No word on my lost keyboard and as I continued to inquire at the front desk, or with the Cruise Director, they slowly but steadily became annoyed with me and actually seemed to enjoy my pain. On the fourth day we arrived in Brunei.

I had found out that there was a plane from Brunei to Los Angeles in the afternoon. I could not miss any more practice so I decided to leave.

After all, I couldn't do a show, so there was no point in staying. I packed up my suitcase of clothes and stuff and got my passport back from the front desk. It was morning and I had some time. I walked off of the ship to look around. On the dock was a local port agent, a native of Brunei, and I introduced myself and recanted my story of woe. He looked at me with deep hatred. His eyes narrowed and then he said, "Finkel, Finkele, Finkelseh. I think I have seen something."

"What? Well, where? How? When? Let's go!" I screamed.

We went to his beat-up Volkswagen and he drove me around the docks. He took me into large airplane hangar-size buildings, bats were hanging; rats were running, but no keyboard case. The rats in Asia dwarf our New York kind. Think Godzilla versus a Chihuahua. We checked all the offices of every building on the dock. Nothing. An hour and a half went by and he said to me, "Please, sorry, we cannot find." I felt a lump in my throat. I knew that was it and I said let's go back to the ship so I can get my stuff and go home.

We drove past a small garbage shed, eight-by-ten building, a wood frame.

"How about in there?" I asked.

"No, no, it is for garbage."

"Please, just let me check it."

"No, it has garbage."

"Sir, in the name of Allah, I beg you to stop." And he did.

I got out and went to the shed. I opened the metal door. In amongst the banana peels, coconut shells, sewage, bugs a'flying and crawlin', there it was. I had no gloves. Without calling my Brunei-guy, I took off my shirt, ripped it in half and wrapped the halves around my hands. I rushed in screaming. I grabbed the case out of the filth. The luggage straps had been opened, but instead of them put back and locked, they had been tied around the case in knots. I guess the local authorities must hate xylophone music. I could tell by the weight, that the keyboard of xylophone bars was in there. I ran out of the shed-Hell and threw the thing in the backseat of the Volkswagen. We returned to the ship.

I opened the case in my cabin toilet's shower. Gentle reader, I'll not disgust you with the particulars that were within. It took a day and a half to clean the keyboard.

The next night I did my show. The audience knew of my plight and applauded wildly at everything. Suckers. I played badly, but I was most entertaining. Maybe the purple suit helped. It took me two weeks to get my hands in shape. My mind has never fully recovered.

Before the ship left Brunei I went back out to the dock to thank the Brunei-guy. He was standing by a small stall where pillbox-style hats were sold. I was ready to give him a tip of fifty dollars and thank him profusely. I went up to the stall and he said, "Mr. Finkeleseh, these are Muslim hats, not for you. Goodbye."

"Wait a minute," I said as I stuffed the fifty dollars down deep into my pocket. "How do you know that I am not Muslim?"

His eyes closed slightly and with a low sneer he answered. "The crew is Muslim. You are American. Jew. Goodbye."

"Tell your king who hires those million-dollar hookers that he ain't no Muslim either!" I shot back.

"No one realizes how beautiful it is to travel until he comes home and rests his head on his old, familiar pillow."
— Lin Yutang

"And puts on one of my CDs" — Ian Finkel

This page has been left blank to give the reader time to cry.

Beat Me Daddy Eight to the Bar
(Grinnell, Iowa - Miami Beach, Florida - Ketchikan, Alaska)

Not all gigs are on cruise ships. I played across the U.S. and abroad and find that there are lousy people all over. Yeah, yeah, there are nice people as well, but I don't find them as interesting to write about and much harder to find.

My dad toured for years and would tell me that it was great to go on the road. Yeah, sure, he was in the legendary First National Company of *Fiddler on the Roof*. All I would get called for is a bar gig in Nacogdoches, Texas. But one time we were on a cross-country tour (I say we, as my band of seven musicians were with me) and after a concert or show, Marty (the great drummer) and I would like to go out to find a place to eat. Not an easy thing for two foodies to do even in this age. Some places just fold their cards after midnight and the motel or hotel stops room service at ten-thirty.

We were in Grinnell, Iowa, performing with the college concert band and they were delightful. Young fresh-faced kids with very decent attitudes and one young lady even baked us a pie! Gooseberry! So good, so delicious! Marty asked her for the recipe and she blushed! I fanned her with one of my CDs. She played bass clarinet, a real sweetie, a peach of a human. We ate it all in between the rehearsal and the concert. I was the star so I took the biggest wedge.

After the gig, Marty and I got into the car we were loaned and set off to find a place to eat. We drove all over the area but everything was, of course, closed. Ready to give up, I suddenly saw a small place that looked open. We had veered off on a side highway and the small lit-up neon sign said Billy O's. Marty went nuts. "Maybe they have some corn chowder; after all, we are in Iowa, or some of that fine corn-fed beef!"

"Marty," I said, "there are a lot of motorcycles in the parking lot, maybe we should pass."

"C'mon, there's food to be 'et!'"

"Oh, all right, but let's be cool when we get in there," I said.

We pulled over and parked. I should say Marty pulled over. He always does the driving and he is the only person in the world I am comfortable with in a car. The man was born with a steering wheel in his hands.

We went into Billy O's. Every guy at the bar had a ponytail, weighed in at over three hundred pounds and their sleeveless arms were covered in large tattoos. There were two pool tables in the back. It didn't take three seconds and the whole joint turned on their seats and looked at us. Well, we were wearing sport jackets and ties; Marty in a light-blue ensemble and me in my normal after-the-show, pink-orange, leisure suit.

A large woman behind the bar cried out, "Boys, you're in the wrong place!"

A moose of a man by the nearest pool table saw us, sneered, spit on the floor and broke his cue stick in half. He must have thought I was Steven Seagal. I got an aluminum taste in my mouth and stage whispered to Marty, "Let's get out of here...fast!"

"Why? Maybe they have some tea and cake," said Marty a bit loud.

Three pit bulls at the bar got up. I heard some glass break and something like, "Tea and cake? Kick their ass, let's get 'em," and other assorted "f" words. I grabbed Marty and pulled him out of Billy O's. We ran to the car, got in and I yelled, "Hit it like my opening number!"

I usually open my show with a crisp quickstep version of the Dixieland classic, "That's a Plenty." Very lively.

Marty, great driver that he is, floored it (while still adjusting his rearview mirror) and off we flew. I looked back and saw a half-a-dozen Harleys in hot pursuit, but they couldn't catch us and we made it back to the hotel and parked. We went into the lobby and the night manager, a Grand-Pappy type, behind the desk said, "What happened at Billy O's?" We were in the sticks of Iowa, but I realized that they did have telephones, though most likely the rotary kind.

"We're going to sleep now," I said. "Is it cool, or are the locals from Billy O's gonna come over and bother us?"

"Nah, those boys were just funnin. You can go to sleep now. . .Did you say you wanted your rooms cool? All you have to do is put on the air conditioner; it will cool off real good."

So our next spot was a safer place. . .Miami Beach. . .a Jewish epicenter. . .or not. Who knew? We finished our concert at a Sunrise Village Condo and it was time to eat. No one told us that two miles down the road was Rascal's, a great deli-restaurant with all the onion rolls you could eat, which is a Jewish requirement. No, Marty stopped the car at a joint on Collins Ave. and said, "This looks good."

I said, "The sign says great German beers. We don't drink."

"True, but I'll bet they've got some great sausage and hot mustard!"

We parked and went in. The place was sparse with few people. No tables, just a bar.

"This is a bar," I say.

"Let's sit and ask."

"Oy," I said.

We sat at the bar. There were only two guys drinking down at the other end. The bartender came over. He looked like the guy who played Goldfinger.

"Yes, Gentlemens!" he said in a heavy German accent.

"What have you to eat?" Marty asked.

"Here, there is no food." I could have swore he clicked his heals. "Just the finest German beers."

"Marty, let's go," I said.

"You gentlemens are from New York, I believe?"

"Yes," I said.

"Ah. . ."

"Whadaya mean?" I said.

Marty shifted in his seat.

"We Germans have a good ear for accents. It must come from our Beethoven heritage."

"Beethoven was deaf," I shot back.

"Well. . .ah, gentlemens, perhaps this is not a place for your kind." I swore I heard his heels click again.

Marty got off of the bar stool and said to me, "He's right, this place is not for us."

"Whadaya mean OUR KIND?" I shot back again. Now I heard him click his heals. The two guys at the end of the bar got up and came over. They looked like Himler and Goering to me.

"Gentlemens, while this area used to be the resort of the Jews, you will now notice that we Germans have occupied the. . ."

I didn't wait for Goebels to finish. (True, the Jews did leave all the great hotels like the Fountain Blue and Eden Rock for the condos but the war has been over for over fifty years!) I grabbed the ex-Auschwitz guard by the collar and pulled him up onto the bar. Marty screamed to me, "What's come over you? Watch your hands!!!"

I was blind with ghetto fury. I dragged old Adolph across the bar like a lion dragging his gazelle-lunch, knocking the two other Germans out of the way. At my destination, which was the other end of the bar, I put my hand on the Nazi's throat and said, "Can't you get used to the fact that every time you start a fight you lose?" Then I slapped him.

Marty looked at the two stunned SS men and said, "Well, I guess you never came up against a xylophone virtuoso before!"

We went back to our hotel and went to bed hungry.

One of our last "land" tours ended in Ketchikan, Alaska, a haven for old hippies that mostly came up here in the late '60s and early '70s. This is a cruise ship port and I told the guys how good it felt not to be on a ship.

None of the band had ever been on one. I have to do the ships alone and use the band that is there due to the fact that the cruise lines will not give me any extra cabins for my guys. So I waved to the cruise ships and took the band out to a local bar. It's a dreary place but it's an American dreary place and we bellied up to the bar, most of the band for drinks, ginger ale for Marty and me. The place was filled with the aforementioned aged hippies and you could see that they instantly hated us. The bartender, a Manson look-alike, took our orders and we got into our usual conversations of cigars, food, and music. Trying my level best to be cool, I turned to see a huge woman on the bar stool next to me. She seemed alone and I instigated a conversation.

"Hello."

She looks at me as if I'm real Denali moose tracks. "Oh, hello," she said.

"Are you from around here?" I asked. You see, I can be provincial, I didn't comment on the City Ballet.

"I am here," she answered, and then added, "Who are you?"

"Ian Finkel."

She cut in and said, "What do you do?"

Now, in the old days, I would have said that I was a xylophonist, or the world's greatest xylophonist, but no one even knows what that is, it's like having a teenager describe a 33 1/3 record or a floor walker, so nowadays I just say I'm a writer. That would open the conversation up a little. But I forgot myself and said, "I'm a xylophonist."

And she replied, "Oh, I went to the foot doctor last week."

Oh, Gabriel, blow your horn.

Marty had a gorgeous Eskimo lady at his side. He was waxing on about the beauty of the land, the lush vegetation, the clean air, and clear glacier waters. I muttered that I wanted to go back to the hotel and stand behind a bus to get my head together. I whispered to Marty, "Why don't you make her one of those pinkie rings out of a fiver, chicks love 'em." And I jabbed him in the ribs. He winked the okay and pulled out a bill. He folded it and twisted it and it became a pinkie ring. He put it on her finger and smiled. I'm so proud of him. The Eskimo lady looked at the ring and took it off. She unfolded it. "Why, this is only a dollar!!" she screamed. "What do you think I am?" One of the boys in the band, who had been watching the coming disaster, said the line, "We know what you are. It's just a matter of price." An old Churchill line and still good, but not good enough for an exit line.

Five big moose-size hippie lumberjacks came over and here we go with the argument. As the voices of the locals and my band got louder, I snuck away and called the hotel. I got our roadie to come over with the free passes to the show; he's big, wooly and looked like them. He talked them down and gave out the free tickets to the concert. Too bad the concert was last night. Free stuff works wonders. The locals gave the band free drinks. Marty and I left in search of Alaskan smoked salmon.

"The populace drag down the gods to their own level."
— Emerson

"Emerson, we finally agree!" — Ian Finkel

This page has been left blank to give you time to cancel your xylophone lessons.

Nut Training
Which is Really Part of Being An Entertainer

Brooklyn in the 1950s was a great place to grow up because everybody was a "character." As a small boy I'd take walks with my father around the neighborhood and stand there as he talked for what seemed like hours to all the nut jobs. After a lengthy conversation on the street (I was always introduced), the character would leave and I'd ask my father who that was. He'd reply, "I don't know." (This, I never did with my children. Maybe I should have.)

Great training to be in show business. But that is the thing about old showbiz types. They'll stop and talk to anyone, the nuttier the better, because they love the attention. As I have said, I do not, but I will talk to anyone for hours on any subject, and if I don't know anything about the topic, I'll lie . . . so what! Everyone leaves happy and I develop my speaking skills.

It teaches you to handle any situation on stage and you'll be surprised who you meet. Even today, my father will grab my hand and thrust it into someone's and say, "Ian, I want you to meet my dearest friend."

He might know them or not. I met a guy once who drove a New York taxi who invented a way to brew his coffee via the heat of his engine. He had the milk in the refrigerated glove compartment that he designed and the sugar, measured I might add, came out of some gizmo on the gearshift. I wish I could attach my espresso machine to my xylophone.

Years later in Hollywood, I met my father for dinner and he thrust my hand into another, saying, "I want you to meet my dearest friend." I shook the man's hand and then saw the face. It was O.J. Simpson. Dearest friend? After all that?!! But I handled it.

I could list the thousands of coo-coos I have met, but here are a few of my favorites.

I was on the New York subway going downtown. Everyone knows there is no smoking on the subway, no one does it, no one ever has done it and no one ever will, but people are nuts about smoking. I was on my way to do a radio show on WNYC and I was sitting on the train reading my *Cigar Aficionado* magazine. It is a hundred-plus pages of nothing and then ten or so pages of great cigars. I was looking at the cigars, which, by the way, all look the same, and a middle-aged lady sat down next to me and said in a bloodcurdling tone, "You're not gonna smoke that thing in here are you??!!!"

"Lady," I answered calmly, "it's a magazine, for God's sake!" How well I behaved.

I told this story on the air and dozens of people wrote or called in saying the same thing happened to them. Example: "I was sitting by the pool and I took out my *Cigar Aficionado* magazine and the guy next to me said, "You're not going to light that thing here, are you??!!"

I was at a Mexican buffet in Las Vegas and a lady came up to me, pointed at a hot plate dish and said, "Young man, what is that?"

I answered, "Why, ma'am, I believe that is Menudo."

"GOD!!! NOOOOOOOO!!!!" she screamed, turned and ran away.

I called to her that she could skip it and go on to the burritos and the charge would still be $6.95, that she didn't have to eat it and I'll protect her and. . .and. . .well, you get the idea.

One night, after a show on a cruise ship, the band and I sat up all night playing poker. When we finally came up for air, it was six a.m. I suggested to all that the buffet was open and I've never seen a breakfast so let's go to it before we went to sleep. We got on line with the passengers and I watched them pile on the morning foodstuffs. There was a couple behind me and I thought I'd give the band some laughs. When I inched my way up to the cereals, I stopped and put seven boxes of Cheerios on my tray. The couple behind me had seen the show and I could tell they wanted to speak to me. They said almost in unison, "Excuse us, Mr. Finkel, but why the seven boxes of Cheerios?"

I answered in my "stage" whisper for all to hear, "I am taking them to Iowa to sell to the farmers as bagel seeds." (Of course, I silently thanked Milton Berle for that joke.) The band screamed with laughter. The wife (I'll tell you how I knew they were married in a minute) shook her head in disgust and said, "Mr. Finkel, we are from Iowa. We grow corn."

The husband chimed in, "I don't believe you can grow bagels. I think you have to bake 'em, like a doughnut."

"That's correct, dear," the wife added. "Remember the Jewish couple we met on the Obscenity of the Seas cruise ship [or whatever ship she said] a year ago? They told us all about bagels."

"And those bialos," hubby said.

"That's right, dear."

I replaced the seven boxes of Cheerios, making a nice pyramid, and was about to say "Bialys," but instead went for the bacon (I didn't eat it) to make them feel at home.

How did I know that they were married? First, let me say that I have seen many horrors firsthand: Disease, murders, torture, plague, sitcoms, IRS audits, but none of them even come close to the ultimate injustice that, the very thought of, sends my stomach juices to a boil.

No matter where I am or how good I feel, I will double over and spit out my pancreas when I see a couple coming toward me wearing the same pink and white, pooty-ooty, zipped up in the front, matching running suits.

It curdles my stomach, my eyes tear and blur. If they are inscribed with "His and Hers" or "Momma and Poppa" or "I'm His - She's Mine," I will eat grass for a month. It never passes. I vividly remember each and every couple that I have encountered, and there have been dozens, to the minutest detail.

And the couple from Iowa had the matching suits on, but with an extra vomitorius addition. Emblazoned across the front of the suits in bold type:

On the man's: DON'T
On the woman's: TOUCH

And on their backs:
On the man's: CORNEY
On the woman's: LOVE

Gentle reader, it would not surprise or disappoint me if you put this book down right now and attempted to regain your composure.

One of my worst nightmares is to play for an audience of thousands, made up of couples in matching running suits. If it did happen for real, though, I am sure my show-business nut-training would take over and I'd charm them, play great, have fun and still be cute. Then, after the show, in my dressing room, I'd vomit for hours.

Show me a thoroughly satisfied man and I will show you a failure." – Thomas Edison

"While I may have failed, I am thoroughly satisfied."
— Ian Finkel

This page has been left blank to give you an opportunity to get out and purchase a Henny Youngman video.

Bands That Should Disband
(Mazatlan, Mexico – St. Petersburg, Russia – Puerto Quetzal, Guatemala – 14th Street, New York City)

From the time I was born (and when I was born I popped out of my mom wearing a tuxedo and I had a cigar in my mouth, and it was lit!) my dad and mom used to drag me, and later they added my brother, to every show up in the Catskill Mountains where my dad worked. You know, the Borscht Belt. My dad was old school in the tradition of Milton Berle, Red Skelton, et al, and had lots of music in his act. All the great comics had music. They sang, danced and had numerous musical cues for the band to play and the bigger the band the better. My dad would point out to us, "Isn't that pianist great?" or, "Listen to that drummer go to town! Whooo!" I couldn't tell at the time, but now I can.

When my dad did the run of *Little Shop of Horrors* for five years, he'd go to the band every night and say, "You are not a band."

The leader-pianist would say, "Of course we are!" (The show's band was a rock-combo consisting of piano, electric keyboards, bass and drums.)

My father, all serious, would then say, "Have you got a trumpet?"

"No, we don't."

"Then you're not a band for public consumption! Get out of the theatre and find a garage!"

Then the musicians would hit the floor laughing as if it was the funniest thing they ever heard. And they heard it thousands of times from him. Musicians always kiss-up to the star. So why do they forever take liberties with me?

So my dad infused into me a love of good musicians and wherever I travel I want to hear the locals play their stuff. Then you'd hear it "right." You don't want to hear some third-rate guitarist from Rumania that sings, who is being accompanied by a God-awful disk, trying to play Salsa. Though that is what it basically has become. Anyone can be a giggin' musician these days, just buy the technology. Dirty rats. It used to be that a musician had to know a lot about music! He had to read, know hundreds of tunes by heart, have a solid technique and be able to play with other musicians of the same ilk. Now? No. Especially on cruise ships in the lounges, one guy or gal with a synth, and, of course, the machines with disks etc. And the people have been dumbed-down to accept those phonies. Now, the show band is another deal. Those are the guys and gals who learn one's act in two hours and do the show. Hopefully. Now and then you do get a bad egg and it's usually the drummer. A band is as good as its drummer, bad drummer, bad band - good drummer, good band. Simple.

Here's another Finkel adage; as technology rises, artistic endeavors go down. Example: There aren't any more Gershwins, Bird, Louis Armstrong or Tchaikovskys around. They have been replaced by disks. Not even a Sousa. To be a good musician, you have to think, not let a machine do it for you. I am considered "unskilled labor." I cannot type at all, so forget about seeing me use a computer. Many friends have tried to teach me the Qwerty keyboard, but, for the life of me, I cannot find the letter "b." Some computer keyboards must be defective. However, I am proud to say, I once was able to do email and after three hours, I got to log onto AOL. Yes, I wrote this book with my quill.

When producers or singers come over to discuss some project they want me to write, they always ask, "By the way, what program do you use? Is it Finale or Sibelius?"

And I tell them, "I use Tchaikovsky."

"Tchaikovsky? Oh. . .Is it new? I've never heard of that program."

"No. It is not new. It's old. A pencil and score pad. Remember the term 'content'? It's not how it looks but how it sounds!"

So, when I first started performing on cruise ships, I'd hang out with the show band. I was excited to go to new places and hear the local bands do their specialty. You learn from them how to play as they would learn from us Americans, our Jazz, and hopefully the technology hasn't poisoned them too much.

And I'm not talking about great virtuosi from other countries. Why, if the equivalent to Rachmaninoff walked into my music room, I'd hit the floor and kiss his fingertips if he'd let me. Not guys like him, I mean the musician on the street. Maybe before the world was so connected by recordings, television etc., you could find some authentic guys playing in a dive somewhere, really making their music, like the Buena Vista Social Club. NOW? Forget-about-it!!! Oh, all right, maybe in a mud hut in Eastern Africa you'll hear something or a couple of Mongolian Monks, but I doubt it.

They all play crap for the tourists. It sickens me. The musicians lowering their art and the tourists lapping it up.

To quote Williams Burroughs: "Squares on both sides."

The first new place for me was Mexico. We left from San Diego. I told the band how excited I was to go and hear the Mariachis play. They snickered at me. We pulled into Mazatlan Port. I saw there was a band on the dock to greet us. I ran off the ship and headed for the band; it is a rather large Mariachi band, plus extra violins and drums. They were hocking out one of the worst renditions of "New York, New York" I have ever heard. I cannot believe my ears! WHY GOD? WHY?

The pianist from the ship came up behind me and tapped me on the shoulder. "I know, I know," he consoled, "you want authentic. Forget it, I've done this run for years; they play down for the American tourists. The suckers are not hip like you, they're Middle Americans. The Mariachis know they'll get more in tips if they play down. 'New York, New York'? Ha! Be grateful it's not 'Memories' from *Cats*, that's the favorite. Come back in an hour and they might play 'La Cucaracha.'"

I did not come back.

Instead, I went to the phone and called my brother, who, though rarely home, was at his place writing. I told him about the Mariachis. He laughed and said "Listen, in my act, I do a New York Medley with '42nd Street' in it and 'Lullaby of Broadway' and 'New York State of Mind' and 'On Broadway' and I end with 'New York, New York.'"

My throat tightened, but I croaked out, "And. . .?"

"The audience loves it! I get a big hand from them. Especially when the stage lights flicker in time to the famous intro."

I hang up.

The morning of the day I was arrested in St. Petersburg, Russia, I was dressed and ready. We were told that a Russian Military band was to greet us on the dock and I told the musicians, "Now, you'll hear those Prokofiev, Shostakovich, et al, marches played right!"

The show band fell over their seats with laughter. "What's so funny?" I asked. They wouldn't tell me. All of them had done that run before and knew the ugly truth.

The ship pulled in. I got off on to the dock and this big, fat, juicy, Russian military band, complete with extra balalaikas, was grinding out "New York, New York."

"Lousy Commie, Rooskie, Bastards!" I cried out. "Where the hell is my man Tchaikovsky? Or Rimsky-Korsakov? Or even Borodin, you freakin' Reds!" I guess you can't protest too much in Russia. Some of the band members looked at me with pity in their eyes.

I went back on the ship to practice some Stravinsky.

Enraged, I found a telephone and called my brother, who was in Australia. I told him about the Russians.

All he said was, "Think about it."

I went back on the ship and practiced some Stravinsky.

Guatemala had a marimba band on the dock. Marimba is the larger cousin to the xylophone. There were four guys on each marimba plus bass and drums. (Imagine if I had three other guys to help me play.) They hadn't started to play and I went over to look at their instruments, which were beautiful. One marimba player recognized me and introduced me around as the "Great Xylophone Soloiste of New-way-va York." Then they played "New York F-cking (you should excuse me) New York."

As the tips avalanched in and though it was impolite of me, I went back to the ship to practice.

When a tour is over, the best thing a musician can do is to forgive and forget. This place had bad food, that place had no coffee, but we survived. As long as the music that we played was together and "right," it was successful. I called up my band and said, "Meet me at 14th Street and Tenth Avenue for some dinner. (Now we're in the real New York!) And the name of the joint is Café Babalu, great Cuban food." Marty got there early and sniffed around. He pronounced the place great and as soon as all the boys were there, he stuck his head in the kitchen and said, "Gentlemen...reload!"

The food was great and halfway through the meal an elderly man dressed beautifully in an old-time, brown, pin-striped, double-breasted suit came in and sat down at the large, ebony, grand piano that was about ten feet from our table. His slacked-down, jet-black dyed hair matched the finish on the piano. This was gonna be good and it was.

The old guy tore into a medley of Lecuona (the great Cuban composer), some Castilian songs and even a piece by Villa-Lobos! We go crazy and all reach into our pockets. There are eight of us all told and we "give it up," ten bucks a head. I put in twenty. I'm the star. I collected the dough and went over to the gent and said, "We're all musicians and we appreciate your artistry...please...accept this," and I gave him the ninety dollars. He weakly smiled, pocketed the tip, and said, "I sorry, Senor, no English, muchas gracias."

"That's all right," and I shoook his hand. As I return to my seat, an electric shockwave went through my eardrums. The old bastard was tearing through a pianistic concerto version of NEW GOD DAMN YORK, NEW PLEASE KILL ME YORK! He's grinning at us, trying to please us and giving it his all. I screamed, "Nooooo! I am not a tourista! I am a musician! Give me my money back!!"

It didn't matter. For the remainder of the night, it was Andrew Lloyd Webber medleys, especially *Cats*, and a two-fisted version of *Les Miz* that made me want to stab my flan.

By the time I got home, it was one in the morning. By four a.m. it was completed. Parts for a ten-piece band in ink and collated.

I had written the greatest drop-dead version of "New York, New York," ever. Since the first caveman hit a log with his club, through the centuries, up to the one-hundredth anniversary of the New York Philharmonic, never, I repeat never, has an orchestrator penned a finer work upon the blessed manuscript paper.

On the next ship, I added it next to closing and, dear reader, if I may be so bold, let me say, I got a standing ovation at the introduction and the audience did not sit down until I begged them to let me go on.

After the show, I went to my cabin and cried for three hours wallowing in self-pity and deep hatred.

"To live a creative life, we must lose our fear of being wrong."
— Joseph Chilton Pearce

"I am never wrong; therefore, I am creative and fearless."
— Ian Finkel

This page has been left blank so you may jot down all the things you like about me.

My Mentor

This is a touchy subject with me, "Musical Mentors." All good musicians will wax on for hours about their teacher, the one who inspired them, the one who took them to jobs to watch and learn, the one who gave a three-hour lesson, the one who made you a pot-roast sandwich, the one who let you sleep on his couch when you were broke, the one who knew everything about your instrument, the one who answered any question on music, never colorizing it with bullshit, the one who advised you on all things: music, food, what to wear, cigars, women. You studied with this person for years, yet it seemed that you never could surpass his excellence, his dedication.

Guys like this are all but gone. If you study with someone now, it's a forty-five-minute lesson, he checks off the page, he barely can demonstrate and then says, "See you next week and pay me now."

I only had two teachers. The first was my mentor and the second was the xylophonist (at the time) in the New York Philharmonic Orchestra. I'll not mention his name. He was a fine player, but a lousy teacher. Forty-five minutes and out. He still owes me four lessons from 1970. He hated me.

I wanted to study with him, as he was the xylophonist in one of the greatest orchestras in the world. The man could play. However, at the lessons, all I could see was a torso and legs behind the *New York Times*, reaching for his Postum and danish. I'd play the hell out of a piece and all he'd say was, "Oh, that'll do'er." Then I'd beg him to demonstrate (not all students can learn this way) and he'd play and I'd try to pick up on his technique. Basically, it was a wordless lesson. You could feel the hatred in the practice room. I guess he was jealous of my talent, I was a better sight-reader, I could play jazz and Latin, he could not. I could play any orchestral excerpt he'd produce at sight. And, I think, most of all, my cuteness bugged him. He called me about three years ago after thirty years, and told me that he'd seen a video of me and wanted to tell me that he thought I played great. I thanked him, of course, but could still feel the pain from the time when my first book came out and I partially dedicated it to him. I called him up to ask him if he enjoyed the copy I had sent to him and he briskly confessed that he had never opened the thing up. Well, I hope he is enjoying his retirement and pension. I heard he doesn't play anymore.

I met my mentor at the Hebrew Educational Society in Brownsville, Brooklyn. My father was teaching the senior citizens acting there. I wanted to play drums, so he enrolled me and got a discount because he worked there (the five-dollar lesson was three bucks) and I was assigned to a man who would turn me into a musician. The drum lessons went on for over an hour and a half, they were supposed to be forty-five minutes, of course, and this teacher wrote everything out on manuscript paper one could imagine. After a year, I went to his house in Manhattan for lessons, they were ten dollars. In his one-room pad on Seventy-First Street he had drums, timpani, vibes and, of course, a xylophone. Though I was basically studying drums with him, he would teach me theory, styles, music appreciation, jazz, Latin, every different kind of music from every country in the world and he had thousands of index cards and records to show examples.

My Mentor   115

He would speak to me at length about the privilege of practice, "Less than five hours a day means nothing." He put up with my bad playing (and switching to trumpet) until I was the age of nineteen. Then he showed me the xylophone and the rest ain't silence.

After I became a pro and went on in my career, I still called him up to ask advice. Funny, he was, for a short time, a student of the xylophonist in the Philharmonic, of course, years earlier, and told me that the guy was a stiff, but to go to him and at least watch him play.

My mentor took me to gigs. He told me about women. I loved him. He's gone now. I wish I could sleep on his couch again.

His name was Norman Grossman.

"For a good man fame is always a problem."
– Graham Greene

"Not by me." – Ian Finkel

This page has been left blank so you can contemplate how YOU started out.

Under the Double Standard
(At Sea - Manhattan, NY - Columbus, Ohio)

I may be the world's greatest xylophonist, but, more importantly, I am the world's biggest comedy fan. I have sat with and interviewed thousands of comedians and I can assure you that what they do ain't easy.

Of course, I am partial to the legendary greats, Milton Berle, Red Skelton, Phil Silvers, Laurel and Hardy, and I could make a list of my favorites, which would be a foot long. I even test the new comics about the old guys and usually they fail miserably. They know nothing pre-Robin Williams. Old comedians sang and danced and many were fine actors. There are plenty of fine new comedians (most don't work the ships, though, more on this later) and I pity them due to the Internet. Some moron hears a joke and retells it (and tells it wrong) and within minutes the whole world knows your act.

A joke I wrote twenty-five years ago for a musicians' convention was about a bronzed rat on a plank. It was just sent to me via the Internet and, as usual, not only was it told wrong it was five paragraphs longer!

Mine: "I walk into a hock shop."

On the Net, twenty-five years later: "A gentleman woke up on a Saturday morning, dressed in his finery, and stepped out onto the street for his morning constitutional." (Constitutional, oh brother!)

Mine: "I see a bronzed rat on a plank, I ask the owner how much it is and he says it's ten dollars, but it's not returnable."

On the Net: "As he walked, ever so briskly, the gentleman was halted by something he had seen through the window of a curio shoppee. It was unusual in nature and certainly caught his eye. The gentleman's curiosity got the better of him and he entered the curio [curio – curiosity! Please kill me] shoppee [shoppee? Isn't that a tribe of indigenous Arizonans?] gingerly and went over to the glass case which housed the oddity. The item in question was a rodent that had been bronzed and then neatly attached to a plank of fine mahogany. The gentleman inquired to the shopkeeper as to its cost and was told that it is thirty-eight dollars and thirteen cents. Also the item is not returnable. [That last sentence was okay.]

Etc.

That gives you an idea as to what is on the Net when it comes to comedy. So comics have it hard today coming up with new stuff. Though the old stuff is still good, new comics constantly write new material for themselves and it is usually not jokes but premises. And they use the "f" word a lot. The cruise ships that I work have a more elderly crowd and they were brought up with jokes: "There was a man standing on the corner, etc." Not premises: "What's with those f-cking cell phones? Can you believe there still is a Macrobiotic restaurant on Broadway?"

And that's the reason a lot of "new" comics do not work the ships. That clientele wants jokes and the ships are deathly afraid of dirty jokes or the "f" word or worse. A blue joke from a comic will get a barrage of bad reports and bad ratings from the guests (except on Carnival Cruise Line, where there is a young crowd and they want that stuff.)

Here's the kicker, the double standard. On cruise ships they have an evening where the guests can win prizes for the worst joke – best joke. The same blue-haired grannies that would stage a protest if a comic went blue or if a comic was *Politically Incorrect* enter these contests. Then, these little old ladies or men tell the most God-awful dirty or racist "jokes" (I don't find them funny at all) you have ever heard! I must say there are wonderful prizes to be won, chipped coffee mugs and slightly damaged computer mouse pads. All prizes have the cruise ship company's logo.

Cruise Director as MC: "And here is Penelope May from Ames, Iowa, and she's eighty-four! C'mon up, Penelope, and tell us your joke!"

Penelope May: "There was the fat lady that stuck her, I mean got her big ol' butt stuck in, I mean on a toilet, and. . ."

Or:

Cruise Director as MC: "And here's Nate Bailey from Eugene, Oregon. C'mon up here, Natey!"

Nate Bailey: "A Jap. . .I mean. . .no, I think she was Chinese. . .went up to see Bill Clinton and. . ."

And? And the audience screams with laughter. Amateur night, a comedy equivalent of Karaoke. Don't get me started. If a comic went that way, he'd be booed off of the stage and never rehired on ships.

I am not a comic. I do not tell any jokes in my act. I'm humorous, charming, and the world's greatest xylophonist. If I told jokes, the audience would expect me to be funny on the xylophone, a la Victor Borge on the piano, nope, no way, not on stage. But I do know thousands of jokes, have a large library of comedy books, references, etc. and I am a riot. I could've been a contender, I mean comedian. I love to tell jokes, but only to the band. They scream with laughter at my stuff and it's not because I give them work. I'll use a guy I hate if he's the best on his instrument.

And you can't tell jokes to regular people anymore. They refuse to laugh or they get into the political correctness like, "Don't do a gag about British coffee, after all, they are our allies and they might be offended and the coffee is grown in Columbia and we are working very hard to. . ." Columbia? Cartagena, maybe.

On cruise ships, I see ventriloquists get away with "showbiz murder." A puppet, a dummy, can say anything. One even said to an audience member, "I'll kick your ass." Can you imagine if a human said that on stage?

(Author's Note: This has nothing to do with comedy clubs, as in those places, if you don't say "F-ck" in every sentence they boo you off of the stage.)

A female guest, on Passenger "Talent" Night, did a ten-minute Lambada dance wearing only two bottle caps and dental floss! (I gave her a standing ovation.)

So, I don't do jokes on stage, only for the band, and we keep laughing.

Late one night in Manhattan at the Burger Joint, I told the gag about a man and his wife having dinner and a young woman comes over and hugs and kisses the man.

Wife:	"Who was that?"
Husband:	"My mistress."
Wife:	"What?"
Husband:	"Look, you got the house, a bucket of jewels, three mink coats, a new Mercedes. . .think it over!"

So she is quiet. Then, at the next table, Mr. and Mrs. Klein (they're in their eighties) are having dinner and a young woman comes over and kisses and hugs Mr. Klein.

Wife:	"Who was that?"
Husband:	"That's Klein's mistress."
Wife:	(After a pause) "You know, we got a prettier mistress than they got!"

The band roared. A lady at the next table turned to me and said, "How dare you tell a sexist joke like that." I wanted to tell her to go on a cruise, but her companion looked like the Hulk so I turned away and talked music all night.

My beautiful half-pound burger with sautéed onions, mozzarella cheese, extra burnt freedom fries and a side of slaw lay ruined.

In Columbus, Ohio, the band and I were in a coffee shop between the rehearsal and show. The jokes were flying. My turn.

Three little old ladies die and go to heaven. An Irish Lady, an Italian lady and a Jewish lady.

(Author's note: You could tell this joke anywhere and end with any kind of lady. Whatever the majority of the audience is or not. It will still get a laugh. If they don't laugh, the hell with them. I'm ending with the Jewish lady.)

Joke continued:

They are met at the gate by Saint Peter. Saint Peter asks the Irish lady, "What can I do for you?"

The Irish lady replies, "I wish to see the Lord."

"Down the hall and turn to the left," Saint Peter answers.

He then asks the Italian lady, "What can I do for you?"

"I wish to see the Lord," she replies.

"Down the hall and turn to the left." Then he asks the Jewish lady, "What can I do for you?"

And she answers, "I, too, would like to see the Lord!"

"Down the hall and turn to the right," he answers.

"Wait a minute! You told the other two ladies to turn to the left!"

"Don't you want to get your hair done first?"

The band roared. The waitress came over to our table and asked me. "Are you Jewish?"

I looked at her and answered, "Yes, I am." She then said, "Well, then, I guess it's all right for you to tell that joke."

Hey! This was a private conversation! Who was she to listen in? Okay, my voice does carry. A stage whisper for me is ninety-five decibels. But, nevertheless, what nerve! But I didn't tell her off, all I did is just turn to each member of the band, one at a time, and there were seven besides me, and said, "No tip. No tip. No tip. No tip. No tip. No tip. NO TIP!!!" And then I looked back at her.

Oh, by the way, if you want to know the rest of the bronzed rat on a plank joke, you can email me.

This page has been left blank so you can perhaps realize what has happened to comedy.

Team Comedy

I must admit, to me, Team Comedy is tops. Can you name anyone you know who publicly admits to seeing all the films of Laurel and Hardy ten times a piece, with their *Sons of the Desert* coming in at least twenty? Abbott and Costello? I have all their films and every episode of their legendary television series, which, I must add, I can do for you verbatim, all the parts and play you the music as well on the xylophone. The comedy of these giants was clean, sweet and, most importantly. . .funny. Where have the teams gone?

I tried to be a team with several other performers, but it never worked out. It always ended up with the other guy saying, "You already have a partner. . .your xylophone!"

So I let that dream go and woke up to the fact that the greatest team ever was on my very lap. My son Abott's two boys, my grandsons, were the very essence of everything that was funny, light and fine.

The older boy, Landen, eleven years old, is a delightful young man full of fun and sweetness and a perfect straight man. The younger of the two, Caley-Jay, possessed the perfect comic spark. He was dedicated to making the world laugh out loud. An immaculate seven-year-old lad whose antics made you fall off of your seat.

Soul mates, linked by the special secret ties of brothers, they were inseparable. I loved them harder than anything that could be described with paper and pen. These brothers held me to a belief of a reality I never imagined could happen.

As any doting grandfather would, I taught them my comedy and it opened up both our worlds to joy and goodness.

Last year, God was feeling low and he needed to shake his blues so he called on Caley-Jay to come up and join him and give the heavens some laughs. The devastation to my family that followed was vast, overwhelming and, of course, these wounds will never heal.

Every time I hear the word "closure," I want to run out into the street and rip up the concrete from the sidewalks until I see the bones of my fingers.

After the funeral, I had to show strength and return to work, though I felt I wasn't ready to entertain. Several weeks went by and I took a ship that left from New York and that is all I remember about it. Who the hell knows where it went to? I was numb; I couldn't eat, sleep or practice music. I kept up my technique with hours of mindless exercises, but every time I tried to play "music" I fell apart. I do not ask you for a medal for getting through the shows. All performers in times of disaster can go on automatic and run on fumes if they must.

I flew from the ship (it was somewhere and I was nowhere) to Hollywood, California, to do the Jerry Lewis Labor Day Telethon. I had done it a year earlier and, believe me, standing in front of that magnificent twenty-piece show band is a thrill that just doesn't come too often in these days of six-piece synthesized groups. I know it went well, Jerry Lewis (he was part of a team) gave me his royal nod, but, I have to tell you, I did not hear a note of the band or my xylophone either.

The year pushed ahead and I used my tepid acting skills to get on. I worked in the Caribbean at Christmas time and returned home for New Year's Eve. The whole family and countless friends were with us in our home, including my son Abott with his beautiful wife Rosa and son Landen, all the family, friends, good wishes. The amazing food and wine had little effect upon me. There was a part of my heart missing that could never be replaced. When midnight came, everyone, of course, exploded and the damn confetti was thrown and the party horns were blasted. Through the blizzard of paper snow, I saw my son look up to the wall where there is a picture of Caley-Jay, his lost boy.

No father, mother or anyone should ever see that expression of the deepest sorrow that can ever be, though many have. My son's face opened my heart and soul's wounds and I lost my addiction to comedy forever.

I cannot watch Laurel and Hardy, Abbott and Costello or any comedy team ever again. My only hope is that my sweet, dear grandson is up there, writing and demonstrating some wonderful funny routines for them to try out in that eternal theater.

> *"Believe me, my young friend, there is nothing, absolutely nothing, half so much worth doing as simply messing about in boats."* – Kenneth Grahame

> *"So, you saw my act?"* – Ian Finkel

> *"Sincerity is the highest compliment you can pay."*
> – Emerson

> *"Unless you're going to put into my show a minimum of $50,000, your sincerity has the value of a three-day-old bialy."*
> – Ian Finkel

This page has been left blank so I may look back.

It's You, You, You
(Somewhere in New Jersey, Brazil, Argentina and Chile)

I hate parties. I feel out of place. I am much more comfortable on a stage with a thousand people staring at me. On stage I rule, at a party I usually spill my plate of chicken paprikosh all over the host. An old pal of mine turned fifty and invited me to his birthday party at his sister's house somewhere in New Jersey. I drove there from Manhattan, where I live, and, as usual, I got lost. As the wrong turns added up, my anger increased and by the time I found the place I was shaking and spitting.

The house was palatial and I figured his sister must be a rich old crone or a richer investment stock-stealing yuppie. I had made up my mind to give my friend his present, a box of Escuro, fifty ring-size, Punch cigars (he just gave up smoking), eat a plate of hors d'oeuvres and get back in the car and go home to safety.

You can't can a kosher ham. I went in and within ten minutes I was holding court. I had a great audience of New Jerseyites and I recounted most of the stories on these pages. Act I was over and at my intermission, I made my way to the restroom, mostly to wipe off the food I had spilled on my new yellow-checkered suit. On the way to the facility, a man came up to me. He lightly tapped my arm and in a very soft but resonate voice, a la a bassoon, introduced himself as the sister's husband, the owner of this Taj Mahal. After the intros, he simply asked me, "Have you ever done any acting?"

I rose up on my toes. "Yes, quite a bit." I was the marimba player in Woody Allen's *Radio Days*. Mr. Allen told his assistant director to ask me to smile more into the camera. Mr. Allen does not speak directly to anyone in the cast unless they are one of the stars. I was not one of the stars. In fact, you can consider this appearance a cameo, because I did not even receive screen credit.

The bassoon continued, "Well, I don't want to talk about myself here at the party, but recently I've written two movies of the week for HBO specials, the last one starring Ellen Burstyn, and currently I am completing a script that. . .that. . .that is *you*."

"Me?" I answered as I felt the blood of showbiz rush through my veins.

"Yes, it's *you*. . .*you*. I have been listening to *you* all night and this new film of mine is *you*."

"I."

"It's about a heavyset (me), Jewish (me), Jerry Lewis-voiced ("lady l'l'lady!") fellow who gets the job coaching a kids soccer team (What's soccer? Never mind!) who has a famous father (that's me), and plays an instrument. It doesn't matter what it is, I mean, I wrote that it's guitar (uh, oh), but it could be the xylophone (Oh yeah!) and his whole demeanor, voice, look, everything is you. *You*! I can't believe it. *You* are the guy I've been writing about. It's amazing. *You* are him!"

"When do I start?"

"I'd like to send *you* a script. I'll work with *you*. When *you* go to see the director, he'll just flip out because it's as if I'd written the whole film for *you*, about *you*. It's *you*!"

I thought quickly and realized something. I confessed, "I just took a nine-week gig on a ship that is going around the bottom of South America, I. . ."

"Don't worry! We don't go into production for four months. I'll send *you* the script. Go. Do the ship. When *you* come back, we'll get together and work the script every day. *You* – are - perfect for the part. Maybe we can get your dad to do a cameo." (My dad doesn't do cameos.)

"He'll play your father! (Hold it! My dad can act rings around me. I'll have to upstage him!) Think of it. The big scene. *You* and your dad on the soccer field. *You* just lost the championship. He humiliates *you*. *You* have a nervous breakdown on the field."

"Wow!"

"And I have a scene at a local bar where your character plays his guitar and thrills the local ladies. I'll change it to xylophone; I bet *you* get an Emmy right out of the box!"

"Sounds wonderful." I had never used the word "wonderful" before.

"Just keep in touch, and I'll get a working script to *you*."

"Fine, fine." I had never used the word fine before either.

The next week went by fast. Marty advised me to trim down a bit. After all, the camera does add ten pounds to your image. I called the bassoon twenty times. He kept up the *you, you,* it's *you* thing. I never got a script and I flew to Rio de Janeiro to pick up the ship. Before getting on, I called him. I called from Buenos Aires. I called from ten ports in Chile from Santiago to Porto Mont to wherever. Each call ended with, "Don't worry; you'll get the script soon. I'll send it to the ship. It's coming out great, etc. etc. because it's *you* – *you* – *you* – *you* hoo - *you*!!!"

I was a big hit on that ship and was offered a fabulous deal to follow, bigger money, better ship, bigger band, the whole thing. I turned it down weighing the two jobs. On one hand was a ship. On the other an Emmy award-winning starring role in a HBO special. I went with the *you* – *you*.

Nine weeks later, I came home. I got my international phone bill, $948.13. I called him up. He only used the *you* – *you* two times. Three calls later, and still no script. The *you* had ceased. Two more calls, and I knew it wasn't going to happen.

The final call was show business perfect. I thanked him for all the *you-yous* and said that I knew that I didn't get the job. In my mind, I thought that most likely they (he) went with a big name, a real star with lots of credits and *you* power. Someone who was like me, but was box office. I swallowed hard and said, "Thanks, anyway. It's okay that I didn't get the part. . .but may I ask *YOU* please. . .who did *you* go with?"

He answered quite simply, "Louis Gossett Jr." I lightly hung up the phone.

Oh, you don't know who Louis Gossett Jr. is? He is a fine award-winning actor, with many film credits. He is a tall, thin, handsome, African American with a winning smile.

He ain't me!

Every performer has a version of this story. All actors, musicians, artists have experienced this story or any one of these stories. Just ask them. In person. Don't email them. Do not download their music. Don't email their jokes told your way. Call them and they'll gladly send you their eight-by-ten glossies, personally autographed and their latest or only CD. It's up to *you*. Because it's *you, you, you. YOU*.

It's You, You, You

"A thing of beauty is a joy forever. Its loveliness increases, it will never pass into nothingness. – Keats

"Are you talking about me?" – Ian Finkel

This page has been left blank,,,, and that is the way my mind usually is.

R-e-s-p-e-c-t
(Thinking Back)

In the dressing room backstage, I'm waiting to go on and do my act. While I check my make-up, my whole theatrical life passes before me as if I am going to die. Then, when I enter the stage, I become reborn. I'd prefer if someone would start an argument with me so I could get all fired up and walk out like the madman I hope I am. But I sit alone and, unfortunately, think.

My first "legit" gig was playing for an off, off, off-Broadway show called *The Happy Hypocrite* (thirty-five years ago at least). I think it ran one or two nights, but during rehearsals my father saw me going to work and stopped me.

"Where are you going?" he asked.

"To the show," I said.

"Dressed like that??!!"

"What do you mean, Dad?"

"You're wearing dungarees and a sport shirt!"

"So what?"

"So what?" he says, "The theater is a holy place. Never go to work without a jacket and tie. It is a place of art, tradition, respect and magic."

"But I'm in the band, nobody sees us."

"Doesn't matter, everything is important, the music, the lights, sound, how you look, it all deserves respect! Go put on a jacket and tie." Then my father flicked the ash from his cigar and sang, "The butcher, the baker, the grocer, the clerk are secretly unhappy men because. . ."

"Dad?"

"The butcher, the baker, the grocer, the clerk, get paid for what they do. . .but no applause. . ." ("There's No Business Like Show Business.")

My father was, as usual, correct. It's all important and should get its proper due. So I try to respect 'em all, but, it's so hard to do that.

In a "real" theater, such as on Broadway, you get everything you need.

On ships? Some of the band is drunk, especially if it's a band from England. It's a pub society and booze is cheap on a ship and they think, that is the way musicians act and don't get me started! 'Cause in New York the musicians come to play - and I mean they eat the music up. I love it when a ship musician screws up my show and then gives me his card so that when he comes to New York I'll use him!

The lighting, sound and stage crew hate it when I give them any stage set-up. They prefer to leave the stage the same way for all the acts and I try to explain, "That's the way I do my act and it is a set-up so no one gets hurt, etc." They turn their backs and walk. So instead of making me comfy, I have to say, "My way or no show!" So they take the lousy five minutes and move the piano and hopefully put the xylophone where it should be.

I remember one night the sound system went off and we had to stop the show until it was fixed (it took ten minutes). I didn't get angry, but after the show no one apologized and the moronic Cruise Director came to me and said, "The show ran long tonight."

"The sound went off and it took ten minutes to fix!"

"You should trim your act."

"You should drop dead!"

All I want to do is go out and entertain the audience, which is not always an easy thing if you're not a household name. Even after a multi-standing ovation show, I'll still get some nut coming up to me and making a stupid comment.

"Excuse me, Mr. Finkel."

"Yes?"

"Your act was okay, but why didn't you play some Floyd Cramer?" (Or Andrew Lloyd Webber, or Disney or whatever?)

"Well, Sir (or Madame), you can't play everything and the things you mentioned really don't fit what I do."

"Well! I mean. . ."

"Didn't you like me?"

"No. I was very disappointed."

"SO-AM-I."

The Stage Damager, an eighteen-year-old boy from Jakarta, who set the stage, calls out, "Two minutes." No five-minute call? No Mr. Finkel? No nothing? I get into position and give a last look at my face in the mirror. I build up my steam and say to the face, "Let me at 'em. I'll kill!"

The announcement is made and the lights come up. The band kicks into my intro. I take a step onto the stage and then I see the horror. They placed my xylophone too close to the curtain (ignoring the tape markings on the floor from the rehearsal) and it is caught on the curtain and is being lifted up, up to the height of at least ten feet. The audience stares in bewilderment and then the xylophone slips off and comes crashing down in front of one and all. The microphones all being on only serve to amplify the ear-splitting sound of my instrument and life being smashed to the floorboards. My poor baby xylophone is a twisted heap. I stand at the side of the stage frozen for a moment and then the curtain comes down.

Half the audience leaves. The rest of the crowd is a jumble of laughter and phony applause. (The show must go on? How? Do I go out and tell jokes? Do my dance? Recite? Striptease?!!)

Not one of the stage crew apologized. Some of the musicians seemed happy to get off early and repair to the bar.

All the Cruise Director could think of saying was, "Oh, let's just show a movie."

I take off my jacket and loosen my tie. I pick up the pieces of my instrument. No one helps.

R-E-S-P-E-C-T?

Exit Music
(My Apartment – Upper West Side of Manhattan, NY)

If you've guessed that I'd prefer to stay home and go to bed and pull the covers over my head, you are wrong. The truth is, I would like to stay home and practice my xylophone eight hours a day and get paid for it. Of course, no one gets paid to practice. Just doctors, I think, so I have to continue my touring.

Some of the musicians and entertainers I know have read this book and have wept openly. Others do not believe a word of it and think I am having a ball seeing the world. Those ladies and gentlemen either have full-time jobs in their local symphony orchestras and can take a cab to work, or in the case of many actors, are doing lucrative voice-overs for commercials tuckering themselves out by reading such heavy copy as: "There's a great deal going on at your local I Hop!"

I do admit that I tried to get into the voice-over business. My father did hundreds of commercials and said, "Try it, it's easy gravy. You never have more than thirty seconds of dialogue. It's not like doing a Shakespearian soliloquy."

So I take lessons with a top voice-over coach, do a demo and she sends it to her agent and the agent calls me up for an interview. I go to her office and she asks me what I am looking for in this part of the business.

I tell her, "I want to do cockroach voices, that's what I am best suited for. In fact, I always dreamed of doing the roach voice for a Raid commercial."

"Well, they already have people for that," she said.

"Maybe they're looking for new faces?" I add.

She doesn't laugh. I shave off my beard and mustache, get new pictures (which cost hundreds of dollars) and continue the lessons. One year later, and I'm still sitting by the phone. So, since I need to work, I'll have to continue my travels. In fact, I have just added a new medley of songs to my act that I would like to run by you. I have assembled a special virtuosic xylophonistic "Tour de Force" that combines "Misty," "The Stars and Stripes Forever," "Memories," the lesser-known arias from Mozart's "Magic Flute" fugued out with the full score of "River Dance," all done to a Salsa beat. Do you think it will work? I hope so because I'm leaving next week on a cruise ship (the S.S. *Moses*, elderly crowd, Kosher meals only) and I want to be the best a xylophonist can be.

Maybe I'll see you on that ship or at one of my gigs in town where the room isn't moving while I play. Come backstage and say hello. My CDs are fifteen dollars each, ten dollars if I autograph them or two for thirty-five dollars.

Wish me "Bon Voyage!" Oh wait, that's French! Just say have a nice time and don't forget to email.

Dedication

"A man's wife has more power over him than the state has."
— Emerson

"And Emmy, old boy, I am glad of it. I dedicate this book to my wife, Cheryl Ann Allen." — Ian Finkel

www.ingramcontent.com/pod-product-compliance
Lightning Source LLC
Chambersburg PA
CBHW071331190426
43193CB00041B/1484